INSIDE A U.S. EMBASSY

HOW THE FOREIGN SERVICE WORKS FOR AMERICA

INSIDE A U.S. EMBASSY

HOW THE FOREIGN SERVICE WORKS FOR AMERICA

Staff

Editor: Karen Krebsbach

Reporters/Writers: Deirdre Fernandes, Nhien D. Le, Laura Ngo

Researchers: Kim Campbell, Michelle R. Tatum

Art Directors: Liz Allan, Tara Fisher

Production Coordinators: Nancy Johnson, Eva-Lotta Jansson

American Foreign Service Association©

2101 E Street, NW

Washington, DC 20037

(202) 338-4045

President: F. A. "Tex" Harris

Executive Director: Susan Reardon

Communications Coordinator: Kristina Kreamer

Cover Map: The Huntington Library, San Marino, Calif.

ISBN: 0-9649488-0-X   ©AFSA, 1996, 2nd ed.

This publication has been made possible through
the generous contributions of:

DACOR

Diplomatic and Consular Officers, Retired (DACOR) is an
association of retired officers of the U.S. Foreign Service, which
was founded in 1952 to promote the welfare and unity of interests of its members and to foster better understanding of U.S. foreign relations. Its governors are also trustees of the DACOR Bacon
House Foundation, established in 1985 to contribute to the development of mutual international understanding and the strengthening of ties between the people of the United States and other
nations. The Foundation's educational outreach activities at the
graduate and undergraduate levels are supported by DACOR
members and their families, largely in remembrance of colleagues
and by bequests and gifts from friends of the Foreign Service.

&

THE UNA CHAPMAN
COX FOUNDATION

Established in 1980 by Mrs. Una Chapman Cox of Corpus
Christi, Texas, the Cox Foundation is dedicated to the proposi-
tion that the United States needs a strong, professional Foreign
Service. It serves that objective by supporting programs and activities to increase public knowledge and understanding of the U.S.
Foreign Service and its role in American foreign policy. The Cox
Foundation also funds career enriching activities for Foreign
Service officers and their spouses, which place them in contact
with the general public. Other Cox Foundation programs address
particular concerns, inherent in service abroad, of Foreign Service
spouses and family members.

&

THE HIRSHORN COMPANY

Providing specialized insurance plans worldwide
as a benefit to AFSA members.

WE SALUTE
THE COURAGE OF THE
U.S. FOREIGN SERVICE

CONTENTS

ACKNOWLEDGEMENTS

Many people contributed a great deal of time, thought and energy to this project, and without their help, this book would not have been possible. They include:

Marshall Atkins, Administrative Officer, U.S. Embassy Canberra
Sheila Austrian, Public Affairs Officer, U.S. Embassy Canberra
Karin Ayers, Community Liaison Officer Assistant, U.S Embassy Cairo
Stephen Barneyback, Defense Attaché, U.S. Embassy Canberra
Mette Beecroft, Cultural Liaison Officer, U.S. Embassy Amman
Kirk Bennett, Political Officer, U.S. Embassy Moscow
Steven Bondy, Economic Officer, U.S. Embassy Amman
Bill Brencick, Political Counsular, U.S. Embassy Buenos Aires
Matt Bryza, Executive Assistant to U.S. Ambassador to Russia Thomas R. Pickering, U.S. Embassy Moscow
Bruce Byers, AFSA Governing Board Representative (USIA)
James R. Cheek, Ambassador, U.S. Embassy Buenos Aires
Margaret Connolly, Foreign Service Secretary, Political/Economic Section, U.S. Embassy Dublin
Michael Corbin, Political Military Officer, U.S. Embassy Cairo
Patricia Crowley, Consular Officer, U.S. Embassy Moscow
William J. Cunningham, Retired FSO
Kathleen Currie, Assistant Editor, *Foreign Service Journal*
Arthur Dornheim, Retired Ambassador
William Duffy, Management Analyst, Office of the Under Secretary of State for Management, U.S. State Department
Wesley W. Egan Jr., Ambassador, U.S. Embassy Amman
Ruta Elvikis, Consul Officer, U.S. Embassy Canberra
Rita Franke, Community Liaison Officer, U.S. Embassy Canberra
Robert Franks, Regional Security Officer, U.S. Embassy Moscow
Carl Gettinger, Political Officer, U.S. Embassy Buenos Aires
Wesley Godard, Community Liaison Officer, U.S. Embassy Buenos Aires
Jo Hahn, Community Lisason Officer, U.S. Embassy Cairo
Nick Hahn, Consul General, U.S. Embassy Cairo
Gabrielle Hampson, Community Liaison Officer, U.S. Embassy Dublin
Jeanie Harris, Foreign Service Spouse and Educator
Mary Ellen Hickey, American Citizen Services Officer, Consular Section, U.S. Embassy Cairo
Tom Huffaker, Economic Officer, U.S. Embassy Moscow
Joseph Huggins, Administrative Counselor, U.S. Embassy Amman
Mark Coolidge Johnson, Science Officer and Acting Counselor, U.S. Embassy Buenos Aires
William Jordan, Political Counselor, U.S. Embassy Amman
Rola Karam, Intern, U.S. Embassy Amman
Michael Keays, Staff Aide to Ambassador, U.S. Embassy Moscow
Stu Kennedy, Director, Oral History Project, Association for Diplomatic Studies and Training, National Foreign Affairs Training Center (NFATC), Arlington, Va.
Karla King, Commercial Officer, U.S. Consulate General Sydney
David Kostelancik, Special Assistant to Ambassador, U.S. Embassy Moscow
Thomas Krajeski, Political Officer, U.S. Embassy Cairo
Ivars G. Kuskevics, Special Assistant, Democracy Programs, Office of the Special Advisor to the President and Secretary of State on Assistance to the New Independent States, U.S. State Department
Alphonse La Porta, AFSA Governing Board Vice President (State)
Samuel W. Lewis, Retired Ambassador
Jeff Lutz, Counselor for Environmental, Scientific and Technical Affairs, U.S. Embassy Buenos Aires

Robin McClellan, Economic Officer, U.S. Embassy Jakarta
Duncan Miller, Mission Deputy Director, USAID, U.S. Embassy Cairo
Ralph Moore, Economic Officer, U.S. Embassy Canberra
Kathleen Morenski, Economic Officer, U.S. Embassy Paramaribo
Judy Murden, Community Liaison Officer, U.S. Embassy Moscow
Ken Nakamura, AFSA Director of Congressional Relations
Kevin M. O'Reilly, Political Section, U.S. Embassy Buenos Aires
Sandra Oudkirk, Vice Consul, Non-Immigration Visa Section, U.S. Embassy Dublin
Oral History Program for Foreign Assistance, Foreign Affairs Oral History Project, Association for Diplomatic Studies and Training, NFATC
Edward Perkins, Ambassador, U.S. Embassy Canberra
Marion Ram, Community Liaison Officer, U.S. Embassy Amman
Jonathan Rice, Cultural Affairs Officer, U.S. Embassy Amman
Warren Robbins, Retired FSO
Elizabeth Rood, Staff Assistant to Ambassador, U.S. Embassy Moscow
Edward Rowell, AFSA Governing Board Vice President (Retirees)
John M. Salazar, Administrative Officer, U.S. Embassy Buenos Aires
Janet Sanderson, Counselor for Economic Affairs, U.S. Embassy Cairo
Christine Speck, Regional Medical Office Nurse, U.S. Embassy Cairo
Michael Speck, Commercial Attaché/FAS Officer, U.S. Embassy Cairo
Paul Shaya, Intern, U.S. Embassy Amman
Jean Kennedy Smith, Ambassador, U.S. Embassy Dublin
Steve Smith, Administrative Counselor, U.S. Embassy Amman
Bob Snyder, Desk Officer for Australia, U.S. State Department
Diana Swain, USAID Deputy Director, U.S. Embassy Amman
Jan Teasdale, Personnel Officer, U.S. Embassy Moscow
Zachary Teich, Economic Officer, U.S. Embassy Canberra
Stephen Telkins, Program Officer, Meridian International Center, Washington, D.C.
Ward Thompson, Retired FSO and AFSA Retiree Liaison
James Truran, Agricultural Counselor, U.S. Embassy Canberra
Leo Voytko, Special Assistant to the Director General, U.S. Department of State
Edward Walker, Ambassador, U.S. Embassy Cairo
Kaarn J. Weaver, Chargé d'Affaires, U.S. Embassy Canberra
Eric Wenberg, Agricultural Officer, U.S. Embassy Moscow
Janet Wilgus, Cultural Affairs Attaché, U.S. Embassy Cairo

SPECIAL THANKS TO:

Raymond C. Ewing, Retired Ambassador, Board of Governors of DACOR (Diplomatic and Consular Offices Retired)
Angela Dickey, AFSA Board of Governors (State), *Foreign Service Journal* Editorial Board
Jess Baily, AFSA Governing Board Vice President (USIA)
Penny Holland, Social Studies Teacher, Williamsburg Middle School, Arlington, Va.
Tom Kelsey, AFSA Governing Board Vice President (FAS)
Richard Thompson, AFSA Coordinator for Professional Issues
Foreign Service Journal **Editorial Board**: Sheldon J. Krys, Chairman; Terrence Brown; David I. Hitchcock; Lisa Bobbie Schreiber Hughes; Mark Matthews; Daniel O. Newberry; Anne Sigmund

A MESSAGE
FROM AFSA

By F.A. "Tex" Harris

In today's world, as America's leadership is being sought around the globe and as U.S. economic competitors are expanding their own diplomatic efforts, a strong Foreign Service is more important than ever. This book provides you, the reader, a rare glimpse into how a U.S. embassy operates, how its many talented and experienced diplomats work together to promote U.S. interests in every embassy and consulate around the world. In this volume, you will also find a collection of contributions from some of our finest diplomats, who have helped make a difference in this world, in foreign policy, in public diplomacy and in development work.

The United States has become a world superpower and leader in large part because of its educated, highly skilled and professional Foreign Service. Why should a distinct Foreign Service exist at all? In a turbulent and rapidly changing world, the United States needs the Foreign Service today much more than it did in 1924, when it was established, or in 1980, when it acquired its current form. For all the profound ways that the world has changed in the last seven decades, the validity of the principle on which the Foreign Service was founded remains undiminished: The need for a corps of dedicated and experienced foreign affairs professionals.

In fact, the case for the primacy of diplomacy in safeguarding U.S. national security and promoting our nation's economic and political interests around the world is stronger than at any time since World War II. With the end of the Cold War, threats to U.S. security are essentially non-military — the result of the disorder and turbulence of a poleless world. Superpower confrontation between the Soviet Union and the United States has been replaced by the liberalizing of trade, ensuring the integrity of U.S. borders, and protecting the global environment. Resorting to the use of military power today is reserved for the defense of narrowly defined "vital interests."

Funds for international affairs programs are not perceived as important, as underscored as by the growing isolationist trend that appears to be sweeping the nation. In the last decade, the U.S. international affairs budget has been halved. Over that same period, the defense budget — about 14 times the size of the foreign affairs budget — was only cut by about 20 percent. Foreign aid, one of the main U.S. foreign policy tools, has also been drastically slashed. From a high of $20 billion in 1985, foreign aid spending fell to $12.4 billion in 1995, representing less than 1 percent of federal spending. Moreover, in real terms, spending for foreign assistance is about 32 percent less than the average level approved by Congress in the late 1980s. Between 1991-95, 17 U.S. embassies or consulates have been closed and 1,100 professionals — predominantly host-country nationals and independent contractors — have lost their jobs. More cuts are planned for the upcoming years.

All of this has been happening as the world has changed dramatically. Since the collapse of the Berlin Wall in 1991, 25 "new" countries have appeared or reappeared, all of which are open to U.S. ideas and investments. As we in the United States have learned from our past, we need to pay attention to the world, since the cost of neglect and ignorance will be higher if we do not. The costs of fighting the forces of totalitarianism during both World War II and the Cold War were extremely high, but the country today cannot afford to turn its back on the world by failing to fund diplomacy, this country's first, most cost-effective and least-risky line of defense in a new and dangerous world.

The us-and-them U.S. foreign policy of the Cold War years is no longer sufficient, as the United States continues it leadership role in addressing the most pressing challenges in the world today: nuclear proliferation; terrorism and international law enforcement; ethnic and religious conflicts; immigration and refugee migration; democracy-building; promotion of free-market economies; management of international rules and norms in hundreds of areas, from air traffic control and telecommunications to food and drug inspection and dual taxation issues; human rights; and environmental concerns, including population growth, disease and pollution.

In the future, the role and the mission of the Foreign Service will extend beyond its traditional responsibilities of reporting, representation, policy recommendation, consular work, development assistance, export promotion, cultural exchanges and public affairs. Since the national interest will always need coherence and balance in foreign policy, a central role of the Foreign Service of the future will be to coordinate and guide American specialists from a variety of agencies and the private sector in the international dimensions of their work. The work of the Foreign Service will encompass all of these undertakings, and more.

America deserves to have the best Foreign Service in the world and AFSA is working hard to ensure that diplomacy is again, as it was in 1924, truly the nation's "first line of defense," and that our U.S. embassies and consulates remain our forward trenches.

As an organization, AFSA has been dedicated to maintaining a strong, effective Foreign Service since 1924, the year both the Foreign Service and AFSA were created. In addition to a professional association, AFSA is also the collective bargaining representative of more than 23,000 active and retired Foreign Service professionals. In this labor-management relations role, AFSA negotiates with the managements of the principal foreign affairs agencies on the working conditions, rights and privileges, and assignment and promotion precepts of Foreign Service employees. It also represents employees in formal grievance proceedings, while providing informal assistance in dealing with administrative problems.

Among the services offered to AFSA members are a program of speakers and conferences on foreign affairs; a scholarship program for the children of Foreign Service employees; a variety of insurance plans; a luncheon club also available for private functions; an on-line program, "Diplomats On Line;" an AFSA World Wide Web page (www.afsa.org); and a four-color, award-winning monthly magazine, the *Foreign Service Journal*. AFSA's corporate affiliates' group, the International Associates, numbering some 45 companies, conducts a standing dialogue among the U.S. international business community, the Foreign Service and the foreign affairs agencies. The general public can become AFSA Associate Members for an annual membership fee. ∎

F. A. "Tex" Harris is the President of AFSA.

WHAT IS THE
FOREIGN SERVICE?

By Karen Krebsbach

Benjamin Franklin, Thomas Jefferson and John Quincy Adams were among America's earliest diplomats, the first representatives appointed by the President of the United States. Later, the diplomatic service evolved into a small and narrowly specialized corps, separate from the consular service, which actively promoted American business, particularly shipping, around the world.

Today's modern Foreign Service, born in 1924 with the fusion of the diplomatic and consular services, now includes about 12,000 U.S. employees and 9,500 foreign nationals at some 165 embassies and 100 consulates abroad. That year, U.S. Rep. John Jacob Rogers of Massachusetts spearheaded the merger with his sponsorship of the Foreign Service Act (Rogers Act), which served to foster a greater sense of *esprit de corps* by folding both groups into a single merit-based recruitment and promotion system. Although Rogers had anticipated the Foreign Service would help fight a coming trade war, security concerns soon eclipsed trade worries as America subsequently became involved in World War II, conflicts in Korea and Vietnam, and the Cold War. Today, trade has again come to the forefront of Foreign Service goals, as personnel become more and more involved in putting U.S. economic interests first at U.S. embassies and consulates abroad.

The need for a corps of educated and trained diplomats was stated eloquently by the drafters of the Rogers Act: "The first responsibility of good government is to safeguard the security of the nation. The first line of defense in achieving this first objective ... is our diplomatic corps and those who direct and back it up in the Department of State. ... Because of the duties and responsibilities they undertake, because of the services they render to American individuals and American business interests, because of their vital role in the conduct of our foreign policy, we in the Congress should demand that the Service be attractive enough to get the highest type of American men and women into its ranks. ... The Foreign Service must compete successfully with other government agencies and private businesses to get the best persons to serve overseas."

Today's Foreign Service employee includes both Foreign Service officers (FSOs) and specialists, and represents a diversity of Americans — white, black, Asian, Hispanic and other ethnic backgrounds — and covers five foreign affairs agencies: the State Department, the U.S. Agency for International Development (USAID), the U.S. Information Agency (USIA) — and its overseas unit, the U.S. Information Service (USIS) — the Foreign Commercial Service (FCS) and the Foreign Agricultural Service (FAS). Frequently, FSOs are assigned to brief tours from one to three years at other agencies, including the National Security Council (NSC), the White House, the Central Intelligence Agency (CIA) and the Department of Defense (DOD).

Foreign Service employees differ from Civil Service employees in their obligation to serve anywhere in the world. Though many qualified applicants apply to the Service after acquiring undergraduate and graduate degrees and language skills, neither a degree nor second language fluency is required to join. Today's FSOs in State and USIA enter the Service by passing a comprehensive written exam and a difficult oral exam. Typically 12,000 take the written exam. In 1995, only 90 new positions were available, a number that varies annually with the agencies' changing needs. The written examination tests an applicant's knowledge of foreign affairs, writing skills and management expertise. Those who pass that test submit to the more difficult oral assessment, which judges an applicant's ability to work with others, and to interpret and report on events. USAID's FSOs enter the system either through an entrance exam or, by virtue of their technical experience, are directly appointed into the system.

Typically, a Foreign Service employee serves for between 18 months and four years at each post in his career, after a period of training in the country's language, history and culture. Though FSOs develop expertise in specific regions of the world, their true specialties are in the skills of diplomacy, communication and negotiation.

Foreign Service specialists enter the Service through a separate process, which emphasizes their particular technical skills and experience. These professionals include communications officers; diplomatic couriers; security officers; information management experts; medical officers and technologists and nurse practitioners; security engineering officers; financial management officers; secretaries; and maintenance personnel.

The United States has been giving foreign aid since after World War II. The Marshall Plan aided Europe's reconstruction. The International Cooperation Agency (ICA), USAID's precursor, was created in 1955 specifically to handle distribution of those funds. USAID was born in 1961, with the express purpose of promoting "U.S. goals through economic development and humanitarian aid," according to the legislation. In 1995, USAID managed $6.1 billion in U.S. foreign aid.

Although USIA was created in 1953 to manage the cultural and information objectives of U.S. diplomacy, its functions have always been an integral part of America's foreign policy program. As noted in a recent agency publication, "It is USIA's mission to strengthen the ties that bind us to all humankind. By increasing mutual understanding between our country and others, you not only uphold a noble ideal, you provide a foundation for international stability, and it is your work that reaffirms the essential spirit of America and provides an umbrella of hope for all." USIA also administers various cultural grants for visiting foreign professors, scholars and other experts through its prestigious Fulbright program.

FCS, as promoter of U.S. economic interests abroad, was created in 1980. FAS, as promoter of U.S. agricultural interests abroad, was moved from the Department of Agriculture to the Department of State in 1939, but was administratively separated again later.

The 1980 Foreign Service Act brought the personnel system of all five foreign affairs agencies under one legislative umbrella. In addition, it created the Senior Foreign Service and established a grievance procedure to assure due process to protect the rights of Foreign Service personnel.

The mission for today's Foreign Service is much more complex than it was in 1924. Today overseas posts promote U.S. policy interests; report on and analyze significant developments in politics and economics, including agricultural trends; maintain good relations with host countries; serve as safe havens and information posts for visiting and resident Americans; screen and process visa and immigration applicants of host country citizens; negotiate international agreements; and interpret U.S. policies and interests for foreign governments, opinion leaders and publics. Its mission is, specifically, to represent America abroad. ■

Karen Krebsbach is the editor of the Foreign Service Journal, *AFSA's monthly magazine.*

U.S. Embassies Around

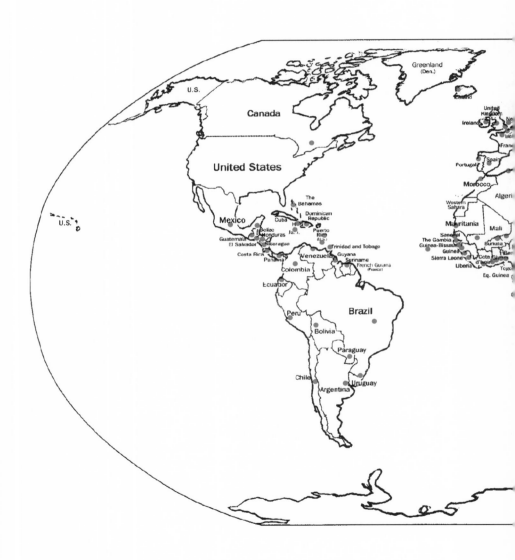

THE WORLD IN 1995

Boundary representation is not
necessarily authoritive

Scale 1:134,000,000
Robinson Projection
Standard parallels 38°N and 38°S

Source: U.S. Department of State, 1995

AFGHANISTAN
  *Kabul (—) (E closed in 1989)
ALBANIA
  **Tirana (E) (Opened in 1991)
ALGERIA
  **Algiers (E)
  Oran (—) (C closed in 1993)
ANDORRA
  *Andorra la Vella (—)
ANGOLA
  **Luanda (E opened in 1992)
ANTIGUA & BARBUDA
  *St. Johns (—) (E closed in 1993; opened in '81)
ARGENTINA
  **Buenos Aires (E)
ARMENIA
  **Yerevan (E) (Opened in 1992)
AUSTRALIA
  **Canberra (E)
  Melbourne (CG)
  Sydney (CG)
  Perth (CG)
  Brisbane (C) (To close in 1996)
AUSTRIA
  **Vienna (E)
  Salzburg (—) (CG closed in 1993)
AZERBAIJAN
  **Baku (E) (Opened in 1992)
BAHAMAS
  **Nassau (E)
BAHRAIN
  **Manama (E)
BANGLADESH
  **Dhaka (E)
BARBADOS
  **Bridgetown (E)
BELARUS
  **Minsk (E) (Opened in 1992)
BELGIUM
  **Brussels (E)
  Antwerp (—) (CG closed in 1992)
BELIZE
  **Belize City (E) (Opened in 1981)
BENIN
  **Porto Novo (E)
BHUTAN
  *Thimpu (—)
BERMUDA
  *Hamilton (CG)
BOLIVIA
  **La Paz (E)
BOSNIA-HERZEGOVINA
  **Sarajevo (E) (Opened in 1994)
BOTSWANA
  **Gaborone (E)
BRAZIL
  **Brasilia (E)
  Rio de Janeiro (CG)
  Sao Paulo (CG)
  Porto Alegre (C) (To close in 1996)
  Recife (C)
  Fortaleza (CA)
  Manaus (CA)
  Salvador da Bahia (CA)
BRUNEI
  **Bandar Seri Begawan (E) (Opened in 1984)
BULGARIA
  **Sofia (E)
BURKINA FASO
  **Ouagadougou (E)
BURMA
  **Rangoon (E)
  Mandalay (—) (C closed in 1980)
BURUNDI
  **Bujumbura (E)
CAMBODIA
  **Phnom Penh (E) (Opened in 1992)
CAMEROON
  **Yaounde (E)
  Douala (C) (Closed in 1993)
CANADA
  **Ottawa (E)
  Calgary, Alberta (CG)
  Halifax, Nova Scotia (CG)
  Montreal, Quebec (CG)
  Quebec, Quebec (CG)

  Toronto, Ontario (CG)
  Vancouver, British Columbia (CG)
  Winnipeg (—) (CG closed in 1986)
CAPE VERDE (Republic of)
  **Praia (E)
CENTRAL AFRICAN REPUBLIC
  **Bangui (E)
CHAD
  **N'Djamena (E)
CHILE
  **Santiago (E)
CHINA
  **Beijing (E)
  Guangzhou (CG)
  Shanghai (CG)
  Shenyang (CG) (Opened in 1984)
  Chengdu (CG) (Opened in 1985)
COLOMBIA
  **Bogota (E)
  Barranquilla (C) (To close in 1996)
  Cali (—) (C closed in 1982)
  Medellin (—) (C closed in 1981)
COMOROS
  **Moroni (—) (E closed in 1993; opened in '85)
CONGO (Republic of)
  **Brazzaville (E)
COSTA RICA
  **San Jose (E)
COTE D'IVOIRE
  **Abidjan (E)
CROATIA
  **Zagreb (E)
CUBA
  *Havana (USINT)
CYPRUS
  **Nicosia (E)
CZECH REPUBLIC
  **Prague (E)
DENMARK
  **Copenhagen (E)
DJIBOUTI (Republic of)
  **Djibouti (E)
DOMINICA
  *Roseau (—)
DOMINICAN REPUBLIC
  **Santo Domingo (E)
EQUADOR
  **Quito (E)
  Guayaquil (CG)
EGYPT (Arab Republic of)
  **Cairo (E)
  Alexandria (CG) (Closed in 1993)
EL SALVADOR
  **San Salvador (E)
EQUATORIAL GUINEA
  **Malabo (E) (Opened in 1981; to close in 1996)
ERITREA
  **Asmara (E)
ESTONIA
  **Tallinn (E) (Opened in 1991)
ETHIOPIA
  **Addis Ababa (E)
FIJI
  **Suva (E)
FINLAND
  **Helsinki (E)
FRANCE
  **Paris (E)
  Bordeaux (CG) (To close in 1996)
  Lyon (—) (CG closed in 1992)
  Marseille (CG)
  Nice (—) (CG closed in 1987)
  Strasbourg (CG)
FRENCH CARIBBEAN DEPT. (Martinique)
  *Port de France (CG) (Closed in 1993)
GABON
  **Libreville (E)
The GAMBIA
  **Banjul (E)
GEORGIA
  **Tbilisi (E) (Opened in 1993)
GERMANY (Federal Republic of)
  **Bonn (E)
  Berlin (—) (BO downgraded from E in 1990)
  Bremen (CG) (Closed in 1986)
  Dusseldorf (CG) (Opened in 1994;

  closed in 1988)
  Frankfurt Am Main (CG)
  Hamburg (CG)
  Munich (CG)
  Stuttgart (CG) (To close in 1996)
  Leipzig (CG) (Opened in 1991)
GHANA
  **Accra (E)
GREECE
  **Athens (E)
  Thessaloniki (CG)
GRENADA
  **St. George's (E) (Opened in 1981)
GUATEMALA
  **Guatemala City (E)
GUINEA
  **Conakry (E)
GUINEA-BISSAU
  **Bissau (E)
GUYANA
  **Georgetown (E)
HAITI
  **Port-au-Prince (E)
HOLY SEE
  **Vatican City (E) (Opened in 1984)
HONDURAS
  **Tegucigalpa (E)
HONG KONG
  *Hong Kong (CG)
HUNGARY
  **Budapest (E)
ICELAND
  **Reykjavik (E)
INDIA
  **New Delhi (E)
  Bombay (CG)
  Calcutta (CG)
  Madras (CG)
INDONESIA
  **Jakarta (E)
  Medan (CG) (To close in 1996)
  Surabaya (CG)
IRAN
  *Tehran (—) (E closed in 1979)
IRAQ
  *Baghdad (—) (E closed in 1990)
IRELAND
  **Dublin (E)
ISRAEL
  **Tel Aviv (E)
  Jerusalem (CG)
ITALY
  **Rome (E)
  Milan (CG)
  Naples (CG)
  Palermo (—) (CG closed in 1994)
  Florence (CG)
  Genoa (—) (CG closed in 1993)
  Trieste (—) (C closed in 1986)
  Turin (—) (C closed in 1988)
JAMAICA
  **Kingston (E)
JAPAN
  **Tokyo (E)
  Naha, Okinawa (CG)
  Osaka-Kobe (CG)
  Sapporo (CG)
  Fukuoka (C)
  Nagoya (C) (Opened in 1994)
JORDAN
  **Amman (E)
KAZAKSTAN
  **Almaty (E) (Opened in 1992)
KENYA
  **Nairobi (E)
  Mombasa (—) (C closed in 1993)
KIRIBATI
  *Tarawa (—)
KOREA, NORTH
  *Pyongyang (—)
KOREA, SOUTH
  **Seoul (E)
  Pusan (C) (Opened in 1984)
KUWAIT
  **Kuwait (E)
KYRGYZSTAN

* *Bishkek (E) (Opened in 1992)
LAOS
   * *Vientiane (E)
LATVIA
   * *Riga (E) (Opened in 1991)
LEBANON
   * *Beirut (E)
LESOTHO
   * *Maseru (E)
LIBERIA
   * *Monrovia (E)
LIBYA
   *Tripoli (—) (E closed in 1979)
LIECHTENSTEIN
   *Vaduz (—)
LITHUANIA
   * *Vilnius (E) (Opened in 1991)
LUXEMBOURG
   * *Luxembourg (E)
MACEDONIA (The Former Yugoslav Republic of)
   * *Skopje (E) (Opened in 1994)
MADAGASCAR
   * *Antananarivo (E)
MALAWI
   * *Lilongwe (E)
   Blantyre (—) (BO closed in 1985)
MALAYSIA
   * *Kuala Lampur (E)
MALDIVES
   *Male (—)
MALI
   * *Bamako (E)
MALTA
   * *Valletta (E)
MARSHALL ISLANDS
   * *Majuro (E) (Opened in 1989)
MAURITANIA
   * *Nouakchott (E)
MAURITIUS
   * *Port Louis (E)
MEXICO
   * *Mexico City (E)
   Ciudad Juarez (CG)
   Guadalajara (CG)
   Monterrey (CG)
   Tijuana (CG)
   Hermosillo (C)
   Matamoros (C)
   Mazatlan (—) (C closed in 1993)
   Merida (C)
   Nuevo Laredo (C)
MICRONESIA
   * *Kolonia (E) (Opened in 1989)
MOLDOVA
   * *Chisinau (E) (Opened in 1992)
MONACO
   *Monaco (—)
MONGOLIA
   * *Ulaanbaatar (E) (Opened in 1988)
MOROCCO
   * *Rabat (E)
   Casablanca (CG)
   Tangier (—) (CG closed in 1988)
MOZAMBIQUE
   * *Maputo (E)
NAMIBIA
   * *Windhoek (E) (Opened in 1990)
NAURU
   *Yaren (—)
NEPAL
   * *Kathmandu (E)
NETHERLANDS
   * *The Hague (E)
   Amsterdam (CG)
   Rotterdam (—) (CG closed in 1986)
NETHERLANDS ANTILLES
   *Curacao (CG)
NEW ZEALAND
   * *Wellington (E)
   Auckland (CG)
NICARAGUA
   * *Managua (E)
NIGER
   * *Niamey (E)
NIGERIA
   * *Lagos (E)

   Kaduna (—) (CG closed in 1994)
   Abuja (BO) (Opened in 1992)
NORWAY
   * *Oslo (E)
OMAN
   * *Muscat (E)
PAKISTAN
   * *Islamabad (E)
   Karachi (CG)
   Lahore (CG)
   Peshawar (C)
PALAU (Republic of)
   * *Koror (E) (Opened in 1988)
PANAMA
   * *Panama City (E)
PAPUA NEW GUINEA
   * * Port Moresby (E)
PARAGUAY
   * *Asuncion (E)
PERU
   * *Lima (E)
PHILIPPINES
   * *Manila (E)
   Cebu (C) (To close in 1996)
POLAND
   * *Warsaw (E)
   Krakow (CG)
   Poznan (—) (CG closed in 1995)
PORTUGAL
   * *Lisbon (E)
   Oporto (—) (C closed in 1992)
   Ponta Delgada (Azores) (C)
QATAR
   * *Doha (E)
ROMANIA
   * *Bucharest (E)
   Cluj-Napoca (BO) (Opened in 1994)
RUSSIA
   * *Moscow (E)
   St. Petersburg (CG)
   Vladivostok (CG) (Opened in 1992)
   Yekaterinburg (CG) (Opened in 1994)
RWANDA
   * *Kigali (E)
SAINT KITTS AND NEVIS
   *Basseterre (—)
SAINT LUCIA
   *Castries (—)
SAINT VINCENT AND THE GRENADINES
   *Kingstown (—)
SAN MARINO
   *San Marino (—)
SAO TOME AND PRINCIPE
   *Sao Tome (—)
SAUDI ARABIA
   * *Riyadh (E) (Upgraded from CG in 1985)
   Dhahran (CG)
   Jeddah (CG) (Downgraded from E in 1985)
SENEGAL
   * *Dakar (E)
SERBIA-MONTENEGRO
   * *Belgrade (E)
SEYCHELLES
   * *Victoria (E) (To close in 1996)
SIERRA LEONE
   * *Freetown (E)
SINGAPORE
   * *Singapore (E)
SLOVAK REPUBLIC
   * *Bratislava (E) (Opened in 1993)
SLOVENIA
   * *Ljubljana (E) (Opened in 1992)
SOLOMON ISLANDS
   *Honiara (—) (E closed in 1993)
SOMALIA
   *Mogadishu (—) (USLO closed in 1994)
SOUTH AFRICA
   * *Pretoria (E)
   Cape Town (CG)
   Durban (CG)
   Johannesburg (CG)
SPAIN
   * *Madrid (E)
   Barcelona (CG)
   Bilbao (C) (To close in 1996)
   Seville (—) (C closed in 1986)

SRI LANKA
   * *Colombo (E)
SUDAN
   * *Khartoum (E)
SURINAME
   * *Paramaribo (E)
SWAZILAND
   * *Mbabane (E)
SWEDEN
   * *Stockholm (E)
   Goteborg (—) (CG closed in 1988)
SWITZERLAND
   * *Bern (E)
   Geneva (—) (BO closed in 1993)
   Zurich (CG) (To close in 1996)
SYRIA
   * *Damascus (E)
TAIWAN
   * Taipei (—)
TAJIKISTAN
   * *Dushanbe (E) (Opened in 1992)
TANZANIA
   * *Dar-es-Salaam (E)
THAILAND
   * *Bangkok (E)
   Chiang Mai (CG)
   Songkhla (—) (C closed in 1993)
   Udorn (C) (To close in 1996)
TOGO
   * *Lome (E)
TONGA
   *Nuku'alofa (—)
TRINIDAD AND TOBAGO
   * *Port-of-Spain (E)
TUNISIA
   * *Tunis (E)
TURKEY
   * *Ankara (E)
   Istanbul (CG)
   Izmir (—) (CG closed in 1993)
   Adana (C)
TURKMENISTAN
   * *Ashgabat (E) (Opened in 1992)
TUVALU
   *Funafuti (—)
UGANDA
   * *Kampala (E)
UKRAINE
   * *Kiev (E) (Upgraded from CG in 1992)
UNITED ARAB EMIRATES
   * *Abu Dhabi (E)
   Dubai (CG) (Opened in 1985)
UNITED KINGDOM
   * *London, England (E)
   Belfast, Northern Ireland (CG)
   Edinburgh, Scotland (CG)
URUGUAY
   * *Montevideo (E)
UZBEKISTAN
   * *Tashkent (E) (Opened in 1992)
VANUATU
   *Port Vila (—)
VENEZUELA
   * *Caracas (E)
   Maracaibo (—) (C closed in 1994)
VIETNAM
   * *Hanoi (E) (Opened as LO in early 1995;
     upgraded to E that same year)
WESTERN SAMOA
   * *Apia (E) (Opened in 1988)
YEMEN (Republic of)
   * *Sanaa (E)
ZAIRE
   * *Kinshasa (E)
   Lubumbashi (—) (CG closed in 1995)
ZAMBIA
   * *Lusaka (E)
ZIMBABWE
   * *Harare (E)

LEGEND	
*Country Capital	(CG) Consulate General
*(E) U.S. Embassy	(C) Consulate
(BO) Branch Office	(CA) Consular Agency
(USINT) U.S.	(USLO) U.S. Liaison Office
Interests Section	(—) No U.S. presence

[1] Fiscal year: See Sources, page 97.

EMBASSY FLOW CHART

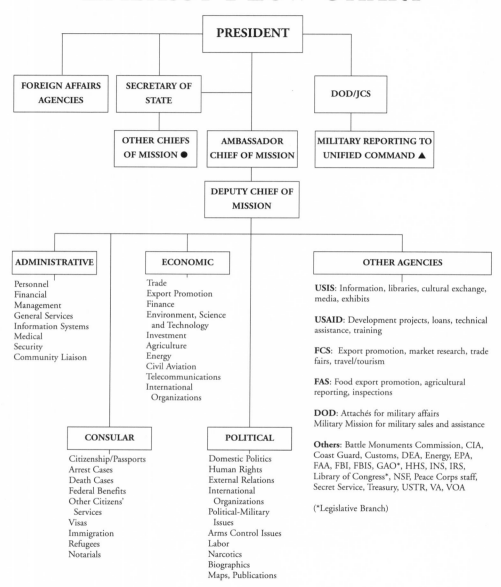

PRESIDENT

FOREIGN AFFAIRS AGENCIES

SECRETARY OF STATE

DOD/JCS

OTHER CHIEFS OF MISSION ●

AMBASSADOR CHIEF OF MISSION

MILITARY REPORTING TO UNIFIED COMMAND ▲

DEPUTY CHIEF OF MISSION

ADMINISTRATIVE

Personnel
Financial
Management
General Services
Information Systems
Medical
Security
Community Liaison

ECONOMIC

Trade
Export Promotion
Finance
Environment, Science
  and Technology
Investment
Agriculture
Energy
Civil Aviation
Telecommunications
International
  Organizations

OTHER AGENCIES

USIS: Information, libraries, cultural exchange, media, exhibits

USAID: Development projects, loans, technical assistance, training

FCS: Export promotion, market research, trade fairs, travel/tourism

FAS: Food export promotion, agricultural reporting, inspections

DOD: Attachés for military affairs
Military Mission for military sales and assistance

Others: Battle Monuments Commission, CIA, Coast Guard, Customs, DEA, Energy, EPA, FAA, FBI, FBIS, GAO*, HHS, INS, IRS, Library of Congress*, NSF, Peace Corps staff, Secret Service, Treasury, USTR, VA, VOA

(*Legislative Branch)

CONSULAR

Citizenship/Passports
Arrest Cases
Death Cases
Federal Benefits
Other Citizens'
  Services
Visas
Immigration
Refugees
Notarials

POLITICAL

Domestic Politics
Human Rights
External Relations
International
  Organizations
Political-Military
  Issues
Arms Control Issues
Labor
Narcotics
Biographics
Maps, Publications

● Austria (UNVIE); Belgium (USNATO), (USEU); Canada (ICAO); France (UNESCO), (USOECD); Italy (FODAG); Switzerland (UN Geneva) United States (USUN), (USOAS)

▲ CINCCENT: Bahrain, Kuwait, Oman, Saudi Arabia, United Arab Emirates. CINCEUR: Belgium, Germany, Greece, Iceland, Italy, Netherlands, Portugal, Spain, Turkey, United Kingdom. CINCPAC: Australia, Cambodia, Japan, Korea, Laos, Marshall Islands, Micronesia, Palau, Philippines, Singapore, Thailand, Vietnam. CINCSOUTH: Honduras, Panama. USACOM: Cuba (Guantanamo).

For a full list of abbreviations and acronyms, see page 96.

Source: U.S. State Department, 1995

CHAPTER 1

WHO WORKS IN AN EMBASSY?

By Dierdre Fernandes

The United States has an accredited Ambassador, the President's personal envoy, in the majority of countries with which it has diplomatic relations. In 1995, the United States maintained a physical presence in the form of an embassy in 164 of the world's 190 countries it recognizes, usually in the capital city. (The United States does not recognize Taiwan and Yugoslavia as nations.) In 1995, America had no diplomatic relations with Iraq, Iran, Bhutan, North Korea and Cuba, although it has long staffed a U.S. Interests Section in Havana.

The key roles of an embassy in a given country include advocating and advancing U.S. policy interests; reporting to Washington on key developments and attitudes within a host country; protecting the welfare of U.S. citizens in the host country; and representing the President, U.S. government and the American people to the host country and its people. Since World War II, U.S. embassies abroad have become bases for up to 40 U.S. government agencies, although Foreign Service professionals represent only about half of government employees at a typical post.

A U.S. embassy may also maintain branches, or consulates, in cities other than the country's capital. Larger branch offices are called consulates general, and are located in major political and commercial centers outside the capital. U.S. representatives also serve at missions at various international organizations, such as the United Nations.

U.S. embassies vary in number of employees. U.S. Embassy Riyadh, in Saudi Arabia, is the largest, with 941 American employees, including hundreds of military personnel. U.S. Embassy Koror, on the tiny West Pacific Ocean island of Palau, is the smallest, with only two U.S. employees. The representatives of all U.S. agencies are collectively known as the country team. Ultimately, every team member is under the supervision of the Ambassador or Chief of Mission.

Embassies include the Political Section, headed by a Political Counselor; the Economic Section, with an Economic Counselor; the Consular Section, with a Consul or Consul General; and the Administrative Section, with an Administrative Counselor. Larger embassies may have a Labor Officer, a Science Officer or a Refugee Coordinator. Some 106 embassies have a USAID presence, with the largest entity — missions — headed by a Mission Director. Some 120 embassies have a USIS office, usually with a Public Affairs Officer, Information Officer and Cultural Affairs Officer. Embassy officials receive critical support services from Foreign Service secretaries, communicators and other specialists, and Diplomatic Security officers. Also important are Foreign Service Nationals (FSNs), usually citizens of the host country, who advise on the local scene and perform many administrative tasks. These profiles of key embassy positions will help readers learn how an embassy team works to advance American interests abroad. ∎

AMBASSADOR

Thomas R. Pickering
U.S. AMBASSADOR TO THE RUSSIAN FEDERATION

The Ambassador is the chief of the diplomatic mission and the personal representative of the President of the United States to the country in which he serves. As Ambassador to the Russian Federation, Thomas R. Pickering, 63, manages all the operations of the embassy and coordinates the activities of the numerous U.S. government agencies that serve American interests in Russia. The Moscow embassy is home to the Departments of Defense, Treasury, Agriculture, Energy, Commerce and Justice, in addition to the main foreign affairs agencies.

As Ambassador since May 1993, Pickering counts himself "fortunate to be [in Russia] at a great time of change. Russia is a country in transition. It is in the process of dismantling its old political and economic institutions and adopting new ones. From establishing a democratic electoral process to its peacekeeping efforts in Bosnia, to promoting world trade by increasing foreign investment activities, Russia is forging a new role for itself on the world stage."

Ambassador Pickering's work day begins early, with Russian language lessons before breakfast. After arriving at the embassy at 8:30 a.m., he reads the many overnight communications from around the world and holds staff meetings of the country team, attended by the heads of each embassy section and agency.

As the day progresses, the Ambassador typically meets with Russian government officials on matters of importance to U.S.-Russian relations and with other representatives of Russian business, science and culture. He frequently also meets with liaisons to American companies doing business in Russia, advising them in gaining access to the Russian market. More than 600 U.S. companies, from McDonnell Douglas to Exxon Corp., are operating in the former Soviet Union, helping to generate $6 billion worth of U.S. trade. And many more are interested in expanding in the region, he said.

Another key issue is U.S. aid to the NIS, the so-called New Independent States, which are former republics of the Soviet Union. This aid peaked at $2.1 billion in fiscal 1995; the U.S. administration's fiscal '96 request was $788 million, although only $641 million was appropriated.

Ambassador Pickering has been especially active in representing the United States beyond Moscow, traveling more than any previous U.S. envoy to that region. So far, he has visited 49 of Russia's 89 areas (equivalent to American states) and nearly every major city. Whenever he travels, he said, he meets Russians who "are eager to expand

*"My experience in Russia has been absolutely fascinating. We seldom
have seen such changes taking place so rapidly — and in the heartland of
a country with which we formerly were in nuclear confrontation."*

business, cultural and educational ties with the United States." Through his frequent
travel and public appearances, Pickering said he accomplishes "one of my most important responsibilities to the President and the American people: encouraging a positive
attitude among policymakers and the Russian public toward the United States."

Pickering also plays host to key U.S. visitors. President Clinton traveled to Russia
in May 1995 for a summit with Russian President Boris Yeltsin; Vice President Al Gore
has been to Russia every year for the continuing work of the Gore-Chernomyrdin
Commission, a Cabinet-level group chaired by Gore and Russian Prime Minister
Victor Chernomyrdin, which is working on eight key bilateral issues, from space and
business to health and defense. Congressional delegations visit Russia frequently to
observe the results of America's cooperative effort in Russia in democratic reform, market economic reform, military conversion and disarmament, space exploration and
technological development. "These visitors show to Russian policymakers and the
Russian people the high value the United States places on a strong relationship with a
stable democratic Russia," Pickering said.

Because the political and economic scene in Russia is rapidly changing, the U.S.
embassy and three consulates under Pickering's purview are undergoing transforma-
tion as well. The embassy is beginning a three-year plan of reconstruction to create a
more functional workspace for the agencies it houses. In 1992, the United States
opened a new Consulate General in Yekaterinburg and, later that year, a Consulate
General in Vladivostok — in Russia's far east.

"I'm privileged to be supervising the change in the embassy from a Cold War-insti-
tution to one of cooperation," he said. "My experience in Russia has been absolutely
fascinating. We seldom have seen such changes taking place so rapidly — and in the
heartland of a country with which we formerly were in nuclear confrontation. This is
good news. For the Russians, there are enormous obstacles to overcome and great hard-
ships in doing so. Our programs of help are very much appreciated and make a serious
difference."

Pickering is a career FSO who holds the rank of Career Ambassador, the highest in
the U.S. Foreign Service. He joined the Service in 1959, after a brief stint in the U.S.
Navy. He has served at the rank of Ambassador since 1974, and as Chief of Mission to
five other countries: Jordan, Nigeria, El Salvador, Israel and India. Pickering has also
served as the U.S. representative to the United Nations and as Assistant Secretary of
State for Oceans and International Environmental and Scientific Affairs.

He holds two master's degrees, one in international relations in 1954 from the
Fletcher School of Law and Diplomacy at Tufts University, and a second in political
science in 1956 from the University of Melbourne in Australia. He also has a 1953
undergraduate degree in history from Bowdoin College. Pickering's hometown is
Rutherford, N.J. ■

DEPUTY CHIEF OF MISSION

Sharon K. Mercurio
U.S. EMBASSY OSLO, NORWAY

C ritical to the diplomatic and operational structure of any embassy is the role of Deputy Chief of Mission (DCM), the mission's second in command. This demanding position requires long hours of work coupled with a keen sense of judgment and flexibility, but it's also "the best job in the world," observed Sharon Mercurio, the DCM at U.S. Embassy Oslo.

Mercurio, 53, oversees a staff of nearly 100, roughly half FSOs and half FSNs. When Ambassador Thomas A. Loftus is traveling outside the country, Mercurio takes over as Chargé d'Affaires, ad interim. She attributes her ability to do the job well to three elements: her management experience, her curious mind and her high energy.

Every work day, she and her staff review and prioritize incoming cables from around the world, deciding whether to recommend to the ambassador any direct action or response. Briefed by the embassy's political and economic counselors twice daily, she and Ambassador Loftus are in constant contact as to actions and reports that may affect U.S-Norwegian relations.

Norway shares a 160-kilometer border with Russia, a fact that has left this Nordic country in a strategic position in terms of U.S.-Russian relations. Currently high on the list of embassy priorities is working with the Norwegian government on a joint project (American, Russian and Norwegian) to expand the low-level nuclear waste treatment facility in northwest Russia, in the Murmansk region. The area is home to Russia's Northern Fleet, which includes 78 nuclear-powered submarines and numerous nuclear-powered surface ships as well as seven civilian nuclear-powered ice breakers. Many of these vessels are being decommissioned and, since Russia lacks adequate facilities and funds to process the resulting waste, the danger is very real that fishing grounds may be contaminated. Norwegians are particularly fearful that the Barents Sea, one of the world's richest fishing grounds, could be at risk. "This project may serve as a model for future international cooperation on nuclear waste treatment," Mercurio said.

Another important responsibility, which Mercurio shares with the Ambassador, is representing U.S. views at a high level to the host government. Security issues high on the agenda include NATO enlargement, an agreed alliance position on the Conventional Forces in Europe Treaty, and Norway's

She attributes her ability to do the job well to three elements:
her "management experience," her "curious mind"
and her "high energy."

participation in the NATO peacekeeping force in Bosnia. Norway is also an important player in other multilateral organizations, particularly the United Nations, and the DCM and her staff seek Norway's support on a wide range of multilateral issues. It was Norway that offered Israelis and Palestinians the secrecy and facility so the two parties could negotiate peace that culminated in a September 1993 agreement. The second agreement between the two parties, known as Oslo II, was signed at the White House in September 1995.

The DCM participates actively in promoting U.S. products, both civilian and defense-related, a major embassy priority. As one of the wealthiest and most developed countries in the world — due to oil and gas reserves — Norway offers enormous opportunities to U.S. exporters. Norway's restructuring of its defense forces, which will focus on upgrading its high-technology equipment, is one such opportunity that the embassy team — the Office of Defense Cooperation, the FCS and the State Department — is successfully pursuing. In 1995, U.S. defense equipment sales to Norway hit nearly $1 billion.

As two committed NATO allies, the United States and Norway have a joint military training program. With a $674 million annual defense fund (nearly 5 percent of GNP), Norway has become a major donor of personnel, equipment and funds to various allied security projects, particularly those of NATO.

Although the United States and Norway have no major diplomatic conflicts, a few "sensitive issues" such as whaling are ever present, according to Mercurio. Norway, Iceland, Russia and Japan are the four remaining whaling nations, despite criticism from the world community. The United States, which shares the world community's anti-whaling position, rarely discusses the issue with Norwegian officials, and has "very little effect on the U.S.-Norway diplomatic relationship," she said.

Having a unified staff is a key reason Mercurio believes her embassy runs so smoothly. She sees her most important role as setting mission priorities, ensuring that all elements of the embassy work together to meet common goals. "With declining resources, that role becomes ever more important," she said. She is the direct supervisor of the Political Counselor and the four FSOs in the Political/Economic Section, setting staff priorities, as well as supervising the Consular Officer and the Administrative Officer.

She joined the Foreign Service in 1976, after 12 years as a Foreign Service spouse. Her previous posts have included Stockholm, Sweden; London, England; Addis Ababa, Ethiopia; and Milan, Italy. She attended Beloit College, the University of Wisconsin-Madison and the University of Grenoble in France, although she never obtained a degree. Her hometown is Edgerton, Wis. ■

POLITICAL CONSELOR

Michele Sison
U.S. EMBASSY ABIDJAN, COTE D'IVOIRE

T he head of the Political Section in an embassy is a critical position, one responsible for reporting to Washington an informed evaluation of political developments affecting the host country; generating support for and actively advancing U.S. policy objectives; and recommending priorities for specific U.S. policy objectives. As the post's expert on political matters, the Political Officer needs to be an expert on the country's history, most importantly its modern political development.

Michele Sison, 36, has been the Political Counselor at U.S. Embassy Abidjan since 1993, heading a small political section of four in this busy embassy in West Africa. Sison also speaks on behalf of the U.S. government to local government officials, political party leaders, private groups and media representatives.

Sison worked doggedly to ensure democratic results for the October presidential and November legislative elections in 1995; the October election drew 56 percent of the voting population and the November vote drew 46 percent. She spent two months preparing for the presidential election and one month readying the embassy for the legislative election. One of her key accomplishments was convincing Côte d'Ivoire government officials to invite 63 international observers, including 20 members of the U.S. mission, whose duty was to certify that elections were fair and representative. This was the first group of observers allowed to witness elections since 1993, when the country's president of 30 years, Felix Houphouet-Boigny, died and was replaced in an election in October of that year by his constitutional successor, Henri Konan Bedie.

Sison said observers were welcomed in 1995 only "after hammering away at the Interior Ministry, which runs the elections, and keeping this issue on the front burner at the U.S. embassy."

Abidjan government officials reversed their stand on election observers only after two years of constant, but low-key pressure by Sison and her staff: In April 1995, President Bedie surprised even his Minister of Interior, Emile Constant Bombet, by announcing that U.N. Secretary General Boutros Boutros Ghali had been invited to observe the elections.

"One reason you need embassies in some of these countries is for this," pointed out Sison. "The same message brought by someone who is covering a

"The same message brought by someone who is covering a country on a regional basis would never have had the same impact at this sort of day-in-and-day-out, week-in-and-week-out message."

country on a regional basis would never have had the same impact as this sort of day-in-and-day-out, week-in-and-week-out message."

In addition, using her contacts with the U.S.-based National Democratic Institute and the International Foundation for Electoral Systems, she was able to arrange many low-key dinner meetings among election observers, Interior Ministry officials and political party representatives — dinners that would help pave the way for more serious, formal meetings that allowed competing parties to discuss major policy issues.

As part of her election preparations, Sison talked to as many voters and political leaders as possible, so she could determine the pre-election mood of the country. This is a key task for political officers in predicting election outcomes accurately.

As Political Counselor, Sison also advises the Ambassador as to which causes USAID should support in Côte d'Ivoire. In 1995, almost $1 million in funds were spent on programs promoted by Sison. This funding came from USAID, as well as the Human Rights and Democratization Fund, which is administered jointly by the State Department, USAID and USIA. Recently, the fund helped support an Ivorian women's group, enabling members to launch a several-year-long civic education campaign to teach women about their voting rights.

One of the projects was a series of sketches and storyboards depicting voting procedures, an effort to educate a population with a 45 percent illiteracy rate in the cities and more than 50 percent in rural areas. Sison said she hopes such voter education programs will "ensure that Côte d'Ivoire continues to be one of Africa's success stories."

Sison's other responsibilities include tracking the development of new and existing political parties in this new democracy, keeping abreast of how the country is expected to vote on various issues before the United Nations, and reporting on human rights issues for the annual State Department report on the subject.

The issues a Political Officer handles have changed in the last two decades, Sison said. "An interesting part of being a political officer now is dealing with these issues of human rights and democratization that were not issues 10 or 15 years ago," Sison said. "You need a never-ending curiosity for why people do the things they do — and try to go after the story like a journalist."

Sison joined the Foreign Service in 1982, the year she graduated from Wellesley College with a B.A. in political science. She has also served in Port-au-Prince, Haiti; Lome, Togo; Porto-Novo, Benin; and Yaounde, Cameroon. She was born in Arlington, Va. ■

ECONOMIC OFFICER

Jay Bruns
U.S. EMBASSY TOKYO, JAPAN

Over the last decade, as U.S. trade policy has become a central focus of diplomatic relations, the role of the Economic Officer has taken on more importance abroad. Working in one of the most critical economic markets in the world, Jay Bruns, 41, serves in the Economic Section of U.S. Embassy Tokyo, having related roles as the Deputy Chief of the Trade Policy Unit and as the embassy's representative to the Asia Pacific Economic Cooperation (APEC) forum.

As Deputy Chief of the Trade Policy Unit, Bruns concentrates on bilateral trade negotiations between Japan and the United States. For example, he was a member of the trade negotiating team that opened Japan's $320 billion insurance market to U.S. insurers in 1994.

Since 1993, Bruns has helped negotiate a number of auto deals more favorable than previous agreements on that especially contentious issue between the two trading partners. For example, his team convinced Japanese automakers operating U.S. plants to purchase U.S.-made parts locally rather than import them from Japan, arguing that the autos would be cheaper to produce and more economically competitive to sell around the world. Similarly, since the United States wants greater access to the Japanese auto marketplace, his team was able to negotiate terms that would allow that, as well as giving Japan slightly more access to the U.S. market. This left both countries' automakers confident they were on "a more level playing field," he said.

The Economic Officer and his staff are also responsible for preparing for U.S. trade delegations that visit the embassy several times a month. "With a trade agenda like ours in Japan, the schedule of visiting officials who are here to either negotiate or monitor existing agreements is excessive," he said. U.S. delegations, with between six and eight members, are now negotiating 16 different economic agreements between the two countries, treaties that cover the gamut from computer chips to whitefish sales. In all these negotiations, Bruns serves as U.S. Embassy Tokyo's representative on the team, which also includes representatives of the Commerce Department, the U.S. Trade Representative's office (USTR), and other agencies, such as the Justice Department. However, the team leader for the American side is usually the USTR representative.

"A great challenge is to convince the Japanese of our arguments, the need for them to take positive steps to open up their economy further. There are a lot of interests that they're trying to protect."

"A great challenge is to convince the Japanese of our arguments, the need for them to take positive steps to open up their economy further," said Bruns. "There are a lot of interests that they're trying to protect, like the agricultural industry — especially apples — and they do that very well. But, our government is insisting on certain changes like fewer barriers to trade and it can become a frustrating experience. It's most welcome when we do reach an agreement and there is a compromise."

Bruns, who speaks Japanese well, usually serves as interpreter between American and Japanese negotiators. He helps to illuminate the subtle contexts behind each English word in the texts, which can number as long as 30 single-spaced pages.

Once the talking begins, Bruns plays a significant role, both in attending negotiations and in communicating constantly with Ambassador Walter F. Mondale, who may be traveling or busy on other issues.

During negotiation of each agreement, Bruns is also responsible for keeping the U.S. delegation informed of daily news of the Japanese economy and political developments. Negotiations for each issue can take upwards of six months, and each point in each agreement sometimes is exhaustively discussed by both parties. Therefore, breaks of up to two weeks are common, a period during which Bruns' job changes again: At this point, he's responsible for using his personal contacts to negotiate one-on-one with members of the Japanese team, trying to determine which issues they're prepared to compromise on and which they're not. His conclusions are cabled to Washington daily, particularly if his findings are relevant to the potential U.S. negotiating position. During breaks, he is also in close contact with U.S. companies doing business in Japan.

In his role as embassy coordinator for APEC, Bruns prepared the embassy for the APEC Summit in Osaka on Nov. 19, 1995, attended by Vice President Al Gore and Secretary of State Warren Christopher.

With the busy economic agenda in Japan, and his staff's usual 11- to 12-hour days, Bruns admitted, "One really does feel useful." He believes the key to being a good Economic Officer is the ability to "make a lot of judgment calls for what is doable."

Before joining the Foreign Service in 1979, Bruns worked on Capitol Hill and was a ski instructor in Colorado. Bruns' other posts have included Oslo, Norway; Bonn, Germany; and Port-of-Spain, Trinidad. He has a 1979 master's degree in international affairs from The George Washington University and a 1976 undergraduate degree in politics from Colorado College. His hometown is Denver, Colo. ■

CONSULAR OFFICER

Adolfo Ramirez
U.S. LIAISON OFFICE SKOPJE, MACEDONIA

The fall of communism sweeping the former Soviet Union and Eastern Europe since 1991 has spawned a growing number of new countries, and in turn prompted the opening of new U.S. embassies, consulates and liaison offices in that region of the world. Since these posts are relatively small, both in physical size and number of employees, they often require one officer to take on the responsibility of two or three jobs. In the two years Consular Officer Adolfo Ramirez, 55, has been at U.S. Liaison Office Skopje, he's taken on additional roles as Administrative Officer and Security Officer.

As Chief Consular Officer, he heads the Consular Section of the embassy, which provides a variety of public services related to travel documents, such as visas for Macedonians visiting the United States and replacement passports for overseas Americans who have lost theirs; handles the protection, welfare and property of U.S. citizens visiting or living in that country; supervises the signing of notarials, public documents and quasi-legal services for Americans; and carries out special services for other U.S. government agencies.

Ramirez was sent alone in February 1991 to the capital of the former Yugoslav Republic of Macedonia (FYROM), supplied with a few thousand dollars, a laptop computer and no knowledge of the Macedonian language. Nonetheless, he negotiated a lease for the liaison office, hired local staffers, and bought furniture, vehicles and communications equipment. The Skopje Liaison Office opened on March 1, 1994. The mission employs 14 FSOs and 40 FSNs.

Ramirez often puts in 15-hour days, six or seven days a week. "If you don't do that, you just don't get ahead soon enough," he said. Since no visa processing equipment exists at the Skopje liaison office, all visas are processed at U.S. Embassy Sofia in Bulgaria, about 150 miles northeast. However, verification of data on visa applications is still done in Skopje, and the information is sent via weekly consular package to Sofia. A driver returns the visas to Skopje the following week. According to Ramirez, the tiny Skopje office processes between 700 and 800 visa requests every year, usually from local government and military officials, as well as artists and teachers, all of whom are interested in visiting the United States for educational, business, diplomatic and, sometimes, medical purposes. Ramirez also negotiates with host government officials those international agreements dealing with consular matters.

Ramirez joined the Foreign Service in March 1981, after spending 10 years as a legislative analyst for the City Council of Los Angeles. His previous posts have included Praia, Cape Verde; Antwerp, Belgium; and Brasilia, Brazil. A native of Los Angeles, he graduated from the University of California in Los Angeles, receiving a B.A. in Latin American Studies in 1970 and a master's degree in international public administration in 1972. ∎

ADMINISTRATIVE OFFICER

Sylvie Martinez
U.S. EMBASSY BELIZE CITY, BELIZE

Each overseas post needs someone in charge of its daily management — or the mission might fall apart — and that job falls to the Administrative Officer. Although U.S. Embassy Belize City Administrative Officer Sylvie Martinez admits it's not a "glamorous" job, she knows it's vital to the embassy's survival. Martinez, 36, has a variety of duties, from managing the finances of an embassy to finding appropriate housing for incoming employees. In her capacity as the financial manager, Martinez pays the bills and makes budgetary decisions, such as recommendations of specific spending cuts and increases in the budget, to the Ambassador. Martinez plans the embassy's $3 million annual budget, and tracks and records expenditures by each department manager. The embassy employs 30 Americans and more than 100 FSNs. She also manages the FSNs, overseeing their hiring and firing, their health and compensation packages, and job description updates.

She is also the primary point of contact for health-related issues for all embassy employees. For example, if an FSO has questions about his insurance coverage, or is not sure if his medical problem warrants being sent back to the United States for treatment, Martinez is the person to approach first. Finding and leasing appropriate and affordable houses and apartments is one of Martinez's most time-consuming duties. When looking for property, she considers many factors, including safety, security and the amount of representational entertaining to be conducted at the sites. Martinez also oversees some computer tasks. Like many non-European posts, U.S. Embassy Belize City has only recently been hooked up for e-mail, which she estimates will save the U.S. government $25,000 a year in long-distance telephone calls. Coming on-line involved a great deal of logistical preparation and Martinez was in constant contact with the State Department, as security and telecommunications issues were being resolved and local technicians were setting up network systems.

Martinez defines her overall embassy role as that of providing administrative support, taking care of details so diplomats can concentrate on the goals of U.S. foreign policy in Belize. She makes sure her colleagues are not worrying about their cars breaking down or termites eating through their homes: That, she says, is her problem. Describing herself as the embassy's "Chief Cook and Bottle Washer," she said her job requires a "tough skin, patience, flexibility and resourcefulness," but she believes she's improving every day.

Martinez joined the Foreign Service in 1982, after graduating with a bachelor's degree in history from the University of California at Berkeley. She also has been posted in Buenos Aires, Argentina; Nuevo Laredo, Mexico; Warsaw, Poland; and Washington, D.C. Her hometown is Sacramento, Calif. ■

ENVIRONMENT, SCIENCE AND TECHNOLOGY OFFICER

Teresa Chin Jones
U.S. EMBASSY OTTAWA, CANADA

Environmental protection issues, science research rights and nuclear arms agreements are an often overlooked and sometimes forgotten aspect of U.S. diplomacy. For example, issues such as which country is responsible for auto emission pollution escaping over a border, are especially relevant in dealing with the United States' friendly neighbor to the north, Canada.

As the Environment, Science and Technology Officer at U.S. Embassy Ottawa, Teresa Chin Jones, 53, acts as a U.S. coordinator and adviser on issues as diverse as water quality, export environmental controls, air pollution, sewage systems and environmental clean-up plans. Jones' main problem is trying to work around rules and regulations "that I have no control over."

Like most FSOs, Jones files regular reports to Washington, and her focus is on Canada's policies on technological development, space programs, technological competitiveness and nuclear arms policy developments. She also assists in bilateral negotiations, such as the U.S.-Canada Air Quality Agreement, flood regulation of Devil's Lake on the North Dakota-Canada border, the U.S.-Canada Boundaries Water Treaty and the Great Lakes Quality Agreement. She also acts as an adviser for pollution control on the Great Lake Quality Agreement. "Canadians understandably have many fears about water pollution in a shared system like the Great Lakes," she said.

Jones also clarifies Washington's views on certain policy issues to Canadian officials, and monitors the environmental aspects of the North America Free Trade Agreement (NAFTA) among the United States, Mexico and Canada. Both the United States and Canada attend the same annual and biannual environmental meetings, such as the Bio-diversity Convention and the International Trade and Endangered Species Convention, so the U.S. government works hard to persuade Canada to support U.S. policy stands on issues such as wildlife protection and conservation. That way, America knows whether its neighbor is also an ally on those issues.

Indeed, Jones pointed out that neighbors sometimes disagree. "Even between the U.S. and Canada, they have two different [political] systems and, therefore,

> *"U.S.-Canadian relations are similar to those of a long-married couple. It's a marriage that has lasted almost 40 years, and they remember almost every argument they've ever had."*

there's room for plenty of misunderstandings," she says. One of those "misunderstandings" came about from a mid-1994 National Academy of Sciences study, which had suggested that the plutonium from U.S. nuclear weapons plants be disposed of at Canada's Deuterium Uranium nuclear power reactor, a site that provides 40 percent of the country's power. After the report's findings were announced, however, Jones had to calm the alarmed Canadians, pointing out that the study was only suggesting the Canadian site be considered as one of several options, and it would not happen until after many years of review and public debate.

The Great Lakes and Devil's Lake treaties, for example, are typical cross-border issues, she says. The two countries are now negotiating not only which one will be paying the bulk of the cleanup and maintenance costs, but also how much each will be responsible for in future monitoring. On both issues, Jones acts as adviser and coordinator, making sure all the parties involved, including engineering experts, state and provincial government officials — and U.S. and Canadian diplomats — receive the proper messages — without cultural or political distortion.

In terms of research on environmental, science and technological issues, Canada and the United States often share their findings and do non-patented research that allows both to jointly take credit. "This cooperation is especially applicable to environmental research, since what affects the United States will sooner or later touch Canada," pointed out Jones. Therefore, if a Canadian researcher is interested in researching the mercury content in the breast milk of a typical Canadian mother, he might call Jones and ask her if she can recommend an American scientist who has done similar studies in the States.

Jones also responds to various requests from Canadian officials, such as how quickly U.S. progress on the information superhighway is moving, or for the names of U.S. companies that sell specific technology products. Long-standing U.S.-Canadian space cooperation is a perfect example of how these allies and neighbors can save money by taking advantage of each other's technology.

"U.S.-Canadian relations are similar to those of a long-married couple," she joked. "It's a marriage that has lasted almost 40 years, and they remember almost every argument they've ever had."

Jones joined the Foreign Service in 1974 after working as a research chemist at a New Jersey chemical engineering company. She received her B.S. and Ph.D. in chemistry from the University of Pennsylvania, and later did post-doctorate work at the Institut Pasteur in Paris. Her hometown is Vineland, N.J. ∎

REFUGEE COORDINATOR

Linda Thomas Greenfield
U.S. EMBASSY NAIROBI, KENYA

M any people have a stereotypical view of refugees as poor, starving Third Worlders. However, Linda Thomas Greenfield, 42, the Regional Refugee Coordinator in Kenya, pointed out that many refugees are well-educated college professors, doctors or lawyers who have been forced to flee political violence or other kinds of chaos in their homelands, which may not necessarily be in the Third World. "It's hard to explain to people that refugees have rights," she says.

Greenfield monitors and reports on refugee situations throughout the 224,960-square-mile country (slightly larger than the state of Texas), and portions of Somalia and southern Sudan. She focuses on refugees' health care and maintenance issues, which entails program evaluation, medical and resettlement assistance, and implementing self-governance programs.

She visits the seven "permanent" refugee camps in her region — usually one a month — and does complete periodic assessments of the three U.S.-funded refugee programs in East Africa. Kenya has two U.S.-funded programs, both run by non-governmental organizations (NGOs): CARE and the International Rescue Committee. She also reports to Washington on regional refugee trends — and political trends that can affect refugees — such as in Rwanda or Burundi, where ethnic conflict produced massive refugee floods between 1993-95.

Greenfield monitors the activities of various refugee agencies, such as the United Nations High Commission on Refugees (UNHCR), the U.S.-sponsored PRO Food Program and the International Committee for the Red Cross. She is also responsible for program evaluations of NGOs that receive U.S. funds through USAID refugee projects, and keeps track of refugee flows among the seven camps. "Even though it's very difficult to track events that could spark refugee flows, these organizations have been quite effective in dealing with the resulting refugee situations," she said.

Handling phone calls from angry or depressed refugees with complaints or demands to be resettled in the United States, is her least favorite aspect of the job. These callers, often village elders whom UNHCR did not consider viable U.S. resettlement candidates, usually ask to meet with her. Beyond these brief encounters, however, Greenfield said, "there's little I can do to help refugees who have been turned down for resettlement. Sometimes my listening makes them feel better. I do what I can."

> *"It's hard to explain to people that refugees have rights. ... Sometimes my listening makes the refugees feel better. I do what I can."*

However, for those 5,000 Africans eligible for resettlement annually in the United States, it's Greenfield's job to coordinate their processing — from application through the flight to the States — with an international migration NGO. Every year for the last few years, between 7,000 and 8,000 East African refugees have requested resettlement in the United States.

The process can take many months. After being prescreened by the Joint Voluntary Agency, applications are sent to the U.S. Immigration Service for review, a process that often requires personal interviews. If the refugee is found eligible for resettlement, after proving he is being persecuted racially, politically or religiously, he undergoes the requisite medical exam — the point at which many get turned down for final approval, according to Greenfield. Roughly 1 to 2 percent of refugees from this part of Africa test positive for the HIV virus that causes AIDS, a diagnosis that immediately disqualifies the applicant unless he can obtain the rare U.S. government waiver. Refugees found ineligible remain in the main Nairobi refugee camp until approved for resettlement elsewhere in Africa or another donor nation, a process that can take up to a year, she said.

Greenfield's job requires close contact with Kenyan government officials, and so she coordinates weekly meetings. She also keeps in touch with her counterparts in the embassies of the world's other major donor countries — Australia, Canada and Britain — to exchange ideas and success stories.

Greenfield is the key U.S. contact person in Africa for the UNHCR repatriation of several thousand Somali refugees to their homeland since civil conflict erupted in the early 1990s, and she acts as the key liaison between the U.S. government and the UNHCR.

She said the results of her efforts are often gratifying, especially when she has noted improved refugee conditions such as higher educational standards, better sanitary conditions and cleaner drinking water, and more self-governance within each refugee community. "But, I also see my share of misery," she admitted. For example, Greenfield was in Tanzania in 1994 when the first Rwandan refugees came across the border, and many were starving. "I saw children die," she recalled. "There is a tremendous malnutrition problem even in the camps here in Kenya. And I see people dying of preventable diseases, like measles and typhoid, the kind of things you just don't expect people to die of in the 20th century."

Greenfield joined the Foreign Service in 1982, after more than a year of teaching political science at Bucknell University. She graduated with a master's degree in political science from the University of Wisconsin-Madison in 1980 and with a bachelor's degree in political science from Louisiana State University in 1978. Her previous posts included Banjul, The Gambia; Lagos, Nigeria; and Kingston, Jamaica. Her hometown is Baker, La. ∎

SECURITY OFFICER

Cliff Flowers
U.S. EMBASSY LONDON, ENGLAND

Of all the major U.S. embassies in the world, London is considered among the safest, a fact that allows visitors to enter the building with a relaxed attitude. For Cliff Flowers, 48, the Security Officer at U.S. Embassy London, maintaining this atmosphere is a challenge. "You have to find the right balance between being security conscious and being paranoid," he said, noting that he is always trying to maintain an equilibrium between those two extremes as he supervises security coverage for the U.S. diplomatic community in London.

Flowers supervises 27 contract guards (mostly British), a 20-person U.S. Marine security detachment, two Regional Security Officers (RSOs) and a security engineer, who handles the embassy's technical security equipment. "That's really an important job at a place like this, since we have no perimeter fence or wall," he said. Instead, the embassy grounds are monitored by a sophisticated computer security system, which allows 360-degree, 24-hour monitoring of every square inch of the compound.

Being on call 24 hours a day, seven days a week has its price, but Flowers finds his job as challenging as it is rewarding. "Frequently I've found that people will come to the security office as the last resort," he said. "We try to show them that we're interested and want to help them, which usually pays off in the long run and they become part of our security family. And you also can't forget that you're a public servant."

One of the most severe security crises Flowers has handled since his arrival was helping to quell 75 demonstrators who broke through the embassy's front entrance in September 1993. The protestors, who were demonstrating against U.S. military involvement in Somalia, were arrested within 20 minutes by U.K. police. "As required under the Vienna convention, we rely on local police to make contact with the bad guys," he said. "It's better for local people to be involved [in the arrest] than American diplomats, even if it's on embassy property."

Flowers is also a member of the Overseas Security Advisory Council, an information-sharing system between the State Department and the U.S. business community worldwide, which helps provide support and information to U.S. business people overseas and "a more secure environment for business," Flowers says. The group, which includes corporate security managers of major U.S. corporations and all the Fortune 500 firms, initiates weekly information mailings and sponsors security conferences on timely business topics such as fraud, which Flowers says is a major problem for U.S. corporations abroad.

"Our intelligence organizations — from the Department of Defense to the CIA — are working very hard on terrorism. They've been using a great deal of resources to try to figure out what terrorists are up to."

In addition to wrestling with key security issues, Flowers has plenty of other details to take care of: conducting investigations of potential and existing employees and FSNs, of thefts reported on embassy property, and of U.S. passport and visa fraud. He also helps to coordinate security arrangements for visiting U.S. dignitaries and officials, in cooperation with U.K. government ministries and the U.S. Secret Service.

Flowers admitted that security planning sessions with U.K. officials, particularly for congressional delegations, can become contentious, since U.K. and U.S. governments hold opposing views on firearms. "There are cultural differences and attitudes towards firearms, and we have very interesting meetings with police and other British officials when we have VIP visits to the U.K.," he said. "Our people normally travel with armed protection, and the Brits don't want to see that here. There are always sensitive negotiations."

Recently, U.K. police were working on a case involving a U.S. citizen who was importing firearms illegally into England. Before U.K. officials could successfully prosecute the individual, they needed information about U.S. law and regulations applicable to this case, data Flowers provided with help from the U.S. Bureau of Alcohol, Tobacco and Firearms.

Flowers' job also requires maintaining cordial relations with the British police, although he said, "We try to take care of ourselves as much as possible." That kind of caretaking includes routine briefings for embassy personnel about community crime — and self-protection in situations such as muggings. Another reason to have a good relationship with local police is to share information, especially on touchy issues like international terrorism. "Our intelligence organizations — from the Department of Defense to the CIA — are working very hard on terrorism," he pointed out. "They've been using a great deal of resources to try to figure out what terrorists are up to." In July 1994, when IRA terrorists set off a cab bomb outside the Israeli Embassy, just across Hyde Park from the U.S. Embassy, Flowers recalled feeling his office shake with the explosion. "A low threat doesn't mean no threat," he said, noting that U.S. Embassy London has never been the scene of a terrorist attack. "This was a reminder that this kind of thing can happen anytime. We still have to keep our eyes open."

Flowers joined the Foreign Service in March 1976 after serving in the U.S. Army for nearly five years. He graduated from Old Dominion University in Norfolk, Va., with a B.A. in history, and later earned the equivalent of a master's degree at the National Defense University, where he studied political, defense and national security issues. His former posts have included Vientiane, Laos; Bonn, Germany; Frankfurt, Germany; Budapest, Hungary; and Lagos, Nigeria. Flowers' hometown is Virginia Beach, Va. ■

INFORMATION SYSTEMS SPECIALIST

Robert D. "Jake" Arriaga
U.S. Embassy Damascus, Syria

In an era when information is power, communication between embassies and the State Department over thousands of miles of land and sea is crucial to implementing U.S. foreign policy abroad. Ensuring that the lines of communication remain accessible is the primary job of the Information Systems Manager (ISM). At U.S. Embassy Damascus, that person is Robert D. "Jake" Arriaga.

The ISM, which Arriaga defines as "a facilitator, a service provider," supervises the maintenance of all communications equipment, including equipment that dispatch telegrams, voices and e-mail; he also manages the diplomatic pouch system — the mail system used by diplomatic personnel. The ISM not only manages the technical equipment in the embassy, but is also responsible for training embassy employees in its use.

In Damascus, Arriaga, 49, works under troublesome conditions, including frequent power surges and outdated equipment, but he makes sure the communication lines between Washington and Damascus are always open. If problems erupt within the telecommunications network, if messages are not received, if questions arise concerning computer programs or telephone sets, Arriaga is the one to call. His clients are primarily embassy employees, although he has been known to help out the Syrian government with answers to an infrequent telecommunications question or two. Arriaga is slowly modernizing the U.S. embassy's telecommunications systems in Damascus, although he admits that task is difficult, given the rapidly increasing technology advances and the rapidly decreasing State Department budget.

Recently, working with the embassy's administrative officer, Arriaga set up e-mail for the embassy, a move expected to save between $3,000 and $4,000 a month in telephone expenses. From Damascus, a phone call to the United States is $5 per minute. "And e-mail can be sent and retrieved at any time, without tying up the embassy's telephone lines," he pointed out.

Arriaga is working toward creating a "paperless office," using desktop scanners almost exclusively to scan paper documents. Each scanner, the size of a loaf of bread, costs $400. Arriaga also has helped start a recycling program whereby the embassy reuses the equivalent of a ream and a half of paper a day. In attempting to bring new technology to the embassy, Arriaga often meets with section chiefs to decide whether to buy certain kinds of communications equipment. "My goal is to standardize computer know-how while cutting costs," he said. "I want to eventually establish a comprehensive and user-friendly networking system."

Arriaga joined the Foreign Service in 1979, after four years in the U.S. Navy and nine years as a police officer in Fremont, Calif. He has taken classes at Chico State University, Ohlone Community College and the University of San Francisco. His hometown is Chester, Calif. ∎

LABOR OFFICER

Thomas Shannon
U.S. CONSULATE GENERAL JOHANNESBURG, SOUTH AFRICA

Reporting on the labor movement allows Labor Attaché Thomas Shannon, a member of U.S. Consulate General Johannesburg's Political Section, a great deal of interaction with the country's citizens on a local level. Although Shannon, 37, also handles labor issues for Swaziland, Maputo, Botswana and Mozambique, his efforts are concentrated on South Africa. He monitors the influence and development of various labor movements, while advancing U.S. labor policy objectives with South African government officials, trade unionists and members of other organizations. His objectives include rebuilding trade relations between workers and company officials in the post-apartheid era, and making South Africa a more attractive country to foreign investors by assisting local governments in restructuring labor regulations and trade policies.

Shannon has found his to be an "extremely exciting job," especially in South Africa, where the influence of labor has been steadily increasing since its influential role in the downfall of apartheid in 1994. "Labor force strength in South Africa is a force of political leadership," he said. "The leaders are highly political figures who are respected in their community. Many new government policies came out of employees' organizations."

South Africa is home to hundreds of labor unions, though only 26 percent of the labor force belongs to one. "Democracy would not exist in this country without trade unions," he said. "Trade unions will play a similar role in the kind of challenges that South Africa faces from today onward, which is, basically, extending democracy from the political realm to the social realm, and making the economy work in a meaningful way." Maintaining contacts with South African unionists and understanding their concerns about political issues are Shannon's main duties. Since trade union leaders, most of whom are well educated, return home at night after day factory jobs to chair local political organizations, Shannon seeks them out in their neighborhoods. Shannon then reports his findings back to Washington, making recommendations where appropriate.

Currently, he is lobbying to amend the country's 1984 Labor Relations Act to include a reference to U.S. interests. These interests may include the promotion of job training for developing industries or the improvement of workers' rights by introducing clauses in their contracts with employers. Shannon works extensively with USIS and USAID to identify key labor leaders to invite to the United States for visits to see how their counterparts live and work.

Shannon joined the Foreign Service in 1984 after earning a Ph.D in politics from Oxford University. He also has a 1982 Oxford master's degree in philosophy and a 1980 B.A. in government and philosophy from the College of William and Mary. Prior to being posted in Johannesburg, Shannon served in Brasilia, Brazil, and Guatemala City, Guatemala. His hometown is San Diego, Calif. ■

MISSION DIRECTOR
(USAID)

Larry Crandall
U.S. EMBASSY PORT-AU-PRINCE, HAITI

Much of the U.S. foreign economic and humanitarian assistance to foreign nations, especially the Third World, is managed by the USAID. Working with individuals, governments and NGOs, USAID supports sustainable development overseas. USAID defines "sustainable development" as economic and social growth that doesn't exhaust resources; that doesn't damage the economic, cultural or natural environments; that permanently increases the society's productivity; and that builds local institutions to empower citizens. One of USAID's most important development assistance projects is in the Western Hemisphere's poorest country, Haiti, which received more than $235 million in U.S. aid in 1995.

As Mission Director, Larry Crandall manages USAID's bilateral assistance programs that provide humanitarian assistance and support for post-crisis transitions; strengthen democratic institutions; improve health, population and nutrition standards; increase broad-based economic growth; and improve the environment.

Haiti most critically needs help in establishing strong democratic institutions. Key USAID initiatives include direct support before and during elections; aid in reform of the judiciary, police and penal systems; and support of existing structures of society, government and legislature. "This is a very important part of what we're trying to do in Haiti," Crandall said. "We're trying to help Haitians help themselves."

For example, USAID provides nearly $13 million annually to support strong democratic institutions worldwide through programs of the United Nations and U.S.-based NGOs such as the National Democratic Institute, International Republican Institute and the American Institute for Free Labor Development. In Haiti, these three NGOs have helped conduct civic and voter education and train poll workers; provide technical assistance to the Electoral Commission; procure ballots and election materials; and monitor elections.

USAID has also provided funds for the retraining of 700 judges, prosecutors and other judicial personnel; the establishing of a new office to monitor judicial performance; the renovating of courts; and the funding of a new police academy. Training by the U.S. Department of Justice's International Criminal Investigative Training and Assistance Program (ICITAP) helped prepare 5,000 new graduates now being deployed nationwide

"[Help in establishing strong democratic institutions] is a very important part of what we're trying to do in Haiti. We're trying to help Haitians help themselves."

and strengthened management structures at the National Police. Other important democracy initiatives include launching a nationwide community self-help program to provide quick response to local needs, and rebuilding and strengthening the national legislature.

As a result of these efforts by USAID, Haiti has witnessed free and fair elections for the first time in its history, taught thousands the skills needed to maintain democracy, and prompted Haitians to empower themselves and become involved in their own development. Says Crandall: "There's been a huge decrease in the number of human rights violations since we began these initiatives."

For USAID, however, the most important resources are human beings. In the area of health, population and nutrition, a comprehensive delivery of services program, carried out by USAID and international organizations such as the Pan American Health Organization (PAHO) and UNICEF, helps up to 2 million Haitians daily by providing vaccinations, oral rehydration salts and family planning assistance. Complementing this effort, USAID manages a daily food program that delivers annually $10 million of U.S. farmers' excess grains and vegetables to 1 million of Haiti's 7 million people.

With regard to broad-based economic growth, assistance is also being provided to push the country's economic recovery plan, which includes supporting a strong business and investment climate, more programs that create jobs, and a strong free-market economy — the foundation of a stable democracy. U.S. officials hope improvement of all three economic factors will raise the standard of living for all Haitians.

Equally important has been USAID's role in protecting Haiti's environment through $20 million to develop environmentally sound agro-forestry activities. If the project succeeds, Haiti would produce enough trees to counter the country's serious deforestation problem.

An important aspect of Crandall's job is maintaining contact with Haitian government officials and top Haitian Cabinet members. For example, he frequently meets with Minister of Finance Jean Marie Cherestal as the pair devise a training stipend program for military officers left unemployed by the dismantling of the Army. These programs help train former soldiers in vocational skills like masonry, computers, electrical wiring and plumbing.

As the key USAID official in Haiti, Crandall is sought after by Haitian government officials as well as visiting U.S. government and business officials. He has helped host President Clinton, Secretary of State Warren Christopher, Deputy Secretary of State Strobe Talbott and a number of visiting U.S. congressional delegations. He is a key source for the international press. Haiti has been one of the world's hot spots for the last few years, and Crandall is the No. 1 person reporters want to interview. "It's been a very interesting time to be in Haiti," he said.

Crandall joined the Foreign Service in 1968, after a two-year Peace Corps stint. His previous posts have included Islamabad, Pakistan; Dhaka, Bangladesh; Addis Ababa, Ethiopia; Kabul, Afghanistan; and Seoul, South Korea. A native of Denver, Colo., Crandall received a master's degree in international affairs from Syracuse University in 1983 and his bachelor's degree in international affairs in 1964 from the University of Colorado. ∎

PUBLIC AFFAIRS OFFICER (USIA)

Nicholas Mele
U.S. EMBASSY KUALA LAMPUR, MALAYSIA

The Public Affairs Officer (PAO) is the chief representative of USIS, the overseas arm of USIA. More than 120 countries have USIS representatives. As Counselor for Public Affairs, the PAO manages the U.S. embassy's public diplomacy, informational and cultural programs, which support and explain official U.S. policies and actions to host country media, government officials and opinion makers. The PAO in U.S. Embassy Kuala Lumpur is Nicholas Mele, 45.

Mele directs his 22-member staff in programs that fulfill the annual USIS country plan, a "contract" approved by the Ambassador, to address public affairs issues that arise in the U.S.-Malaysian relationship. The fastest-growing member of the Association of Southeast Asian Nations (ASEAN), Malaysia already has drawn a total of $8 billion in U.S. investment — a figure growing 18 percent annually. Malaysia is a politically stable, parliamentary democracy with a long-standing commitment to free trade. Its abundant natural resources, especially natural gas and oil, and its educated population helped generate more than $14 billion in exports to the United States in 1994, mostly sophisticated high-technology products and industrial goods. That year, Malaysia was the 13th largest exporter to the United States.

Effective public diplomacy helps shape how Malaysians perceive the United States, its government and policies. Mele, his Information Officer (IO), Cultural Affairs Officer (CAO) and their Malaysian staffs develop and implement the programs that maintain a positive dialogue with influential Malaysians in government, academic, media, business and cultural institutions.

This outreach work includes the International Visitor program and other exchange programs. Under the auspices of USIA, a visitor spends 30 days in the United States, meeting his professional counterparts and learning about other aspects of American society and life. One of the program's most successful features is the "home hospitality" aspect whereby American volunteers invite visitors to their homes for a meal and, in some cases, an overnight stay. Malaysian candidates are selected for the program by a Mission committee and interviewed by the CAO to determine his or her interests and availability. Mele or the CAO briefs each International Visitor before his departure and, upon return, they follow up with a series of meetings.

Mele and his staff use state-of-the-art communication technology to link USIA in Washington, D.C., with dozens of American databases, allowing the USIS staff to respond rapidly to specific requests from Malaysian contacts, predominantly reporters. "Access to

"In my experience, it's relationships between people, visits to one another's home countries, which are the most effective and long-lasting method of creating and expanding mutual understanding."

Internet is critical to the success of USIA's mission to 'tell America's story to the world,'" Mele said. "It opens a conduit between the embassy in Malaysia and Washington D.C., where communication of facts and information vital in policymaking can be exchanged more quickly."

Likewise, when Malaysian government officials express concern about such issues as how ethnic relations are managed in the United States, Mele's staff is able to provide a variety of facts and informed American opinion as well as the latest U.S. government policy statements. The same is true if the question involves U.S. policy and actions toward North Korea's undeclared nuclear arms program, U.S. relations with Vietnam, the social and political standing of members of the Islamic faith in America, or a host of other questions that influence the bilateral dialogue.

Working with his IO, Mele tries to overcome misconceptions about Americans and the United States fostered in the Malaysian media by providing Malaysian journalists with a variety of information on key topics of interest. (Although there is little anti-American sentiment in Malaysia, unbalanced media coverage portrays an America under siege by gangs and violence and where the majority of Americans are dying of AIDS.) The basic tool is a daily "Wireless File" of U.S. government policy statements and policy background information compiled by USIA in Washington, D.C., and transmitted electronically to USIS posts around the world.

The IO and his staff analyze the major Malaysian daily newspapers and television news broadcasts to see how U.S. policies and actions are being reported. Malaysian media commentary on important bilateral, regional and world affairs in which the United States has a key stake — deployment of U.S. troops in Bosnia, for example — is reported to Washington.

Mele also employs another public information instrument to inform key audiences in Malaysia about U.S. policies and values: American speakers. With the help of USIA/Washington, he invites American government and academic experts to Malaysia to address important topics in dialogues with government officials and private-sector leaders. The speakers' program and non-academic and academic exchanges are, in Mele's words, "the backbone of everything we do." One reason there is so little anti-American feeling in Malaysia, he says, is because more than 100,000 Malaysians have earned degrees at U.S. universities. "We need to try to foster some linkages between American and Malaysian think tanks, universities and scholarly institutions," Mele says. "In the U.S. relationship with Malaysia, as in our bilateral relationships with other nations, commercial or political dealings are not sufficient glue to bind the relationship. Educational links and exchanges of people and information are essential." Says Mele: "In my experience, it's relationships between people, visits to one another's home countries, which are the most effective and long-lasting method of creating and expanding mutual understanding."

Mele joined the Foreign Service in 1975. He received a B.A. in English literature from Columbia University in 1972 and briefly attended Georgetown University's School of Foreign Service, not completing his degree before being assigned to his first Foreign Service post. His previous posts have included Pretoria, South Africa; Kumasi, Ghana; Seoul, South Korea; and Surabaya, Indonesia. He is a native of New York City. ■

CULTURAL AFFAIRS OFFICER
(USIA)

Gloria Lloyd
U.S. CONSULATE GENERAL RIO DE JANEIRO, BRAZIL

Brazil, with its huge cities of Brasilia, Rio de Janeiro, Recife and Sao Paulo, has one of USIS's largest and most diverse cultural programs. The primary goal of USIS programs is to build better understanding of American culture, values and society to support U.S. foreign-policy objectives. The Cultural Affairs Officer (CAO) at U.S. Consulate General Rio de Janeiro is Gloria Lloyd.

Lloyd, under the direction of Country Cultural Affairs Officer Dennis Donahue at U.S. Embassy Brasilia, is responsible for coordinating a mix of American speakers, artists, cultural presentations and art exhibits in Rio de Janeiro, the country's largest city. Brazil is the world's fifth-largest country in terms of area, with 150 million people spread out over a region as large as the 48 contiguous U.S. states. Brazilians' principal heritage is Portuguese, African or a mixture of the two. Many people have Italian, German, Japanese and Arab blood as well.

Lloyd, 45, loves the diversity of her position. "On a typical day I may deal with a government official seeking information on how American private institutions and the U.S. government fund the arts," she said. "I may also be in touch with a university professor trying to find an American academic to participate in a foreign-policy conference. Or I might work with a Brazilian-U.S. binational cultural center offering space for an American photo exhibit or introduce a performance by two American classical guitarists visiting Brazil as 'Artistic Ambassadors.'

"Actually, there are no typical days when our subject matter is as broad as all of America and the audience is as large and varied as Brazil's," she said. Although most of Lloyd's efforts are focused on the arts, economics is an important issue as well. "I have to decide, for example, the most appropriate kind of program in promoting U.S. interests," she said. "For a local Chamber of Commerce it may be the benefits of a more open trading regime; for an invited audience of bankers it may be how the U.S. regulatory system supports financial markets; for a university graduate program it may be modern management systems in the U.S."

For long-term projects, Gloria may call upon USIA/Washington to send an academic or cultural specialist to work with a Brazilian host institution. An American specialist is recruited to address a specific issue identified by USIS. While a speaker may spend two weeks in the country, a specialist can spend up to six weeks at one institution providing American expertise to a major Brazilian cultural or educational organization. In 1995, USIS Brazil programmed 100 speakers and specialists on various topics. Most speakers were recruited by USIA in

> *"American culture has many facets. We try to show as many of them to Brazilians as we can. Our responsibility is to fulfill American foreign policy goals. Culture helps us do that."*

Washington, while others were invited to participate in USIS programs during their own visits to Brazil. "Speakers and specialists perform a labor of love when they participate in USIS programs," Lloyd said. She noted that speakers are free to express a diverse range of opinions, receive travel and living expenses and a $100-a-day honorarium. "They do it not for money but for the opportunity to share their experiences in the U.S. with Brazilians and to make professional contacts often continued for a lifetime. This is the value of exchange. It's not a one-time event but part of a process that may beneficially affect Brazilians' perceptions and thinking about the United States over a long period."

For an invited audience of bankers, Lloyd may turn to electronic programming. Through the USIA Worldnet satellite television network, Brazil sponsored 10 Worldnet teleconferences on topics varying from defense to urban renewal. In her work at a university, Lloyd may recommend an educational exchange to a faculty member, directing him to the Fulbright program operated by a U.S.-Brazilian commission in Brasilia. Funded primarily by USIA, America's premier academic exchange program in Brazil is also funded by the government of Brazil and American and Brazilian businesses. In 1995, 67 Brazilians received Fulbright assistance for study and teaching in the United States and 35 Americans studied in Brazil.

Lloyd believes that the deepest and most accurate impressions of the United States are the result of spending time in America, noting that USIA sponsors two programs for professional visits to the United States: the International Visitor Program and the Voluntary Visitor Program. In the first, foreign leaders are hosted by USIA for visits up to 30 days, while they meet and exchange ideas with their U.S. professional counterparts, attend cultural activities and other kinds of programs. In 1995, USIS Brazil sponsored 61 visitors, from fields as diverse as culture, academia and business. In the second program, the Voluntary Visitor Program, Brazilians traveling to the United States for tourism or business are offered a U.S.-coordinated itinerary, such as appointments with counterparts in their fields. In 1995, USIS Brazil assisted 58 voluntary visitors.

For a CAO, the day is seldom over. At night, Rio is alive with operas, ballets, symphonies and other musical performances, exhibits and poetry readings. It's part of Lloyd's job to make sure that American artistic creativity is showcased in this rich cultural environment. In 1995, she organized performances in Rio by the American black, female a capella group, "Sweet Honey in the Rock." But the performance wasn't just about music: Lloyd hosted key Rio residents after the concert for a discussion of race, welfare and AIDS in Americans' lives.

Lloyd also works with public and private galleries and theaters, as well as the 50 Brazilian-American binational centers that highlight the Brazilian-U.S. artistic and cultural relationship. Although each center is independent, operated by Brazilians and self-funded through English classes, USIS assists with U.S. cultural programming and the services of several consultants.

Lloyd joined the Foreign Service in 1980. She graduated in 1972 with a bachelor's degree in communications and in 1975 with a master's degree in advertising and public relations, both from Michigan State University. Her previous USIS postings have been in Belgrade, Yugoslavia; and Accra, Ghana. Her hometown is St. Joseph, Mich. ∎

COMMERCIAL OFFICER

(FCS)

Judy Reinke
U.S. EMBASSY BONN, GERMANY

It's not unusual to hear American businesspeople note the difficulty in establishing overseas markets for their products, but several U.S. government agencies have been partners at the forefront of that struggle for nearly 100 years. A key client of the State Department and the Commerce Department overseas is the U.S. businesspeople. Although commercial work abroad had been performed by State's Economic Officer or Commercial Officer for many, many decades, in 1980 the Foreign Service Act authorized the moving of those FSOs from State into the personnel and assignment system at the U.S. Commerce Department. Still, the work remained the same.

"My client and Commerce's client is American business, who have the legitimate right to U.S. services, both domestically and overseas," said Judy Reinke, 36, the Commercial Officer for FCS in Bonn, Germany, and does double duty as the embassy's Commercial Attaché. She represents the United States on a macro or policy level, focusing on policy advocacy of U.S. interests in the various trade bodies, like the World Trade Organization (WTO) or the Organization for Economic Cooperation and Development (OECD).

In her duties as Commercial Attaché, Reinke was instrumental in preparations for the New Traditions Conference in September 1994 in Berlin. This conference, the brainchild of former Ambassador to Germany Richard Holbrooke (more recently Assistant Secretary of State for European Affairs), was meant to symbolize the continuity of the U.S. mission to Germany in a post-Cold War era and to emphasize the role of commerce in U.S.-German diplomatic relations. According to Reinke, this emphasis shift helped American firms become more involved in U.S. foreign-policy interests.

As the mid-level officer in Bonn's commercial section, Reinke focuses on the practical and microeconomic issues of the economic relationship between the two countries. She supervises market research for U.S. companies, developing plans to determine which industries and economic sectors should be researched for eventual entry, and handles briefings for visiting U.S. business representatives. For example, U.S. trade specialists in Berlin recently completed a market analysis for pre-fabricated housing kits. The report, which found the economic climate ripe for U.S. makers of housing kits, will be submitted to the Commerce Department and sent to the National Trade

"My client and Commerce's client is American business, who have the legitimate right to U.S. services, both domestically and overseas. ... I think it's a very important mission."

Data Bank to be used by U.S. exporters interested in exporting such kits. "We help American companies find the right German partner," she said. "We're the big arm of the American market here."

Already, thousands of American companies are successfully exporting to Germany everything from computer chips to autos; however, those companies with German-based offices or factories only number in the hundreds.

Every year Reinke coordinates the dozen U.S.-sponsored trade fairs in Germany covering various economic sectors. She also writes customized market analyses for U.S. companies that specifically request data on prospects for exporting a vast array of products, from canned food to clothing.

One of Reinke's key roles is as a consultant for American companies having trouble entering the German market. Usually small and relatively new, these companies often need a little extra help coping with exporting to a foreign market. In coordination with the embassy's economic section, Reinke argues on behalf of these companies, and will also help develop an export strategy. She points out that her role as Commercial Officer is not to compete with international consulting firms, but rather "to provide an affordable and timely introduction to business market research for small- to medium-sized businesses." "Most of them don't yet have an overseas agent."

One of the sectors Reinke has targeted for U.S. business is energy. So far, Germany's public-owned energy sector has been closed to foreign investment. U.S. companies, however, have shown great interest in purchasing, building and operating electric power plants in eastern Germany, she said.

Although the Commercial and Economic Sections of an embassy may appear synonymous to an outsider, there are striking differences in the type of reporting each section does, according to Reinke. The Economic Section basically reports on market and general economic trends in the host government's economy, focusing on bilateral trade policy and macroeconomic policy. The Commercial Section, on the other hand, examines the German market to determine how to best serve its clients: U.S. companies.

Furthermore, unlike the Economic Section, the Commercial Section is budgeted and supervised by the Commerce Department, not the State Department. FCS shares the mission of the Department of Commerce to promote U.S. exports abroad. "It is important that people focus on the fact that Commerce is really helping U.S. business to expand and grow overseas," she said. "I think it's a very important mission. I feel like I have been involved in making those clients feel like they have somebody to turn to."

Reinke joined the Foreign Service in 1993, although she has been with the U.S. Department of Commerce since 1983. Bonn is her first Foreign Service post. She graduated in 1980 with a bachelor's degree in government from Smith College and received a master's degree in public administration from Princeton University's Woodrow Wilson School in 1983. She is from Fairfax, Va. ∎

Agricultural Officer
(FAS)

Thomas Hamby
U.S. Embassy Stockholm, Sweden

Working in the Baltics and eastern Scandinavia as the Regional Agricultural Counselor for the FAS, Thomas Hamby acts as the liaison between the U.S. government and those of Estonia, Latvia, Finland and Sweden, which altogether buy $350 million in U.S. agricultural and fishery exports a year.

"I think I can play the middleman between the countries to facilitate both understanding and trade, which are the glues that cement the countries together," said Hamby, 48. As the Agricultural Counselor, Hamby's key goal is helping U.S. traders and businesses to export a wide range of agricultural, fish and forestry products. The region is an active trading partner with the United States:

■ In fiscal 1995, Estonia imported $41 million in U.S. agricultural, fish and forestry products. The major U.S. products purchased by Estonia were $25 million worth of poultry and $9 million worth of coarse grains. Estonia sells about $1.3 million worth of agricultural, fish and forestry products to the United States annually, primarily wood products and cheese.

■ Latvia imported $9.5 million in U.S. agricultural, fish and forestry products in fiscal 1995. Major imports were $1.7 million in wine and beer, $1.4 million in poultry meat; and $1.4 million in forestry products. Latvia exported $3.5 million worth of agricultural, fish and forest products to the United States in fiscal 1995, primarily dairy and forest products.

■ Sweden imported $182.7 million in U.S. agricultural, fish and forest products in fiscal 1995. Most imports were processed fruits and vegetables ($37.8 million), tree nuts ($20.9 million) and fish products ($18.5 million). Sweden exported $126.3 million worth of agricultural, fish and forest products to the United States in fiscal 1995, primarily roasted and instant coffees and forest products.

■ Finland imported $83.3 million in U.S. agricultural, fish and forest products in fiscal 1995. Major imports were $11.6 million worth of processed fruits and vegetables and $10.3 million worth of poultry meat. That year, Finland exported $91.5 million worth of agricultural, fish and forest products to the United States, primarily coarse grains, cheese and forest products.

One major issue Hamby has wrestled with in the last year has been the impact on agricultural exports of integration of Sweden and Finland into the trade bloc of the European Community (EU), which also includes France, United Kingdom, Germany, Italy, Portugal, Spain, Greece, Italy, Austria, Belgium, The Netherlands, Luxembourg and Denmark.

> *"Direct contact with key policymakers in individual member capitals like Helsinki and Stockholm is vital to achieving U.S. trade policy goals in negotiations with the EU."*

Estonia and Latvia are recognized as non-voting associate members of the EU, receiving favored access to its market. Although the United States strongly supports EU's expansion, it also must watch its own trade interests, Hamby said. Although most U.S. negotiating is done at the EU headquarters in Brussels, "direct contact with key policymakers in individual member capitals like Helsinki and Stockholm is vital to achieving U.S. trade policy goals in negotiations with the EU," he said.

The EU is a critically important factor in U.S. commercial relations in Europe and is often the subject of Hamby's reports. Although the EU is a U.S. ally, its trading bloc is one of the United States' main competitors in the world, which poses a particularly thorny challenge to U.S. diplomats overseas. "It's necessary to find a balance between supporting the integration of the Baltics and other countries into the EU and legitimate U.S. trade interests that are harmed by the adoption by these countries of EU trade-oriented policies, which we are opposing right now in various ways," said Hamby. "We support and recognize Sweden and Finland joining the EU but at the same time, always encourage the reduction of trade barriers through, for example, international trade agreements like the Uruguay Round and the World Trade Organization. We do not encourage countries to adopt duties or other trade-impeding practices that would give unfair trade advantages and move away from a free market."

One of Hamby's recent reports considered the application of EU support programs that raised the price farmers can receive for some kinds of grains, and which in turn can prompt increased production of grain that will have to be a subsidized export, thereby unfairly competing with U.S.-grown grain and other non-subsidized grain exporters.

Hamby is working to ensure U.S. access to the former Soviet Union via Helsinki, which he called "the perfect gateway into the Russian market," because of its sophisticated transportation system. Since the collapse of the Soviet Union in 1991, the New Independent States and the rapidly democratizing states of Eastern Europe have shown growing appetites for Western products. Hamby believes that "the United States should take advantage of those markets," he said. With the aid of trade flow analyses and trade export statistics, in 1994 alone, he noted an 80 percent increase in the U.S. poultry and fish exports that has passed through this "gateway."

Problems with market access related to trade policy aside, promoting U.S. agricultural products involves intense multifaceted efforts, such as organizing and participating in trade shows, and in making contacts between foreign buyers and U.S. sellers. For example, Hamby's office recently participated in a trade show on expanding U.S. exporters' knowledge of the emerging markets in the former Soviet Union. "One of our best efforts has been the highly successful promotion of FAS's Trade Leads Program, which involves identifying buyers and potential buyers for U.S traders," he said. The program helped promote $31 million of U.S. agricultural products in fiscal 1995 alone.

Hamby joined FAS in 1977, after a year administering the Tennessee Department of Agriculture. He holds a 1974 B.A. in economics and a 1976 M.S. in agricultural economics from the University of Tennessee. His former posts have been Moscow, the Russian Federation; Taipei, Taiwan; and Tokyo, Japan. His hometown is Maryville, Tenn. ■

Foreign Service Secretary (All Agencies)

Kathryn Walsh
U.S. Embassy Pretoria, South Africa

The Foreign Service Secretary is the glue that holds together an embassy, a USAID mission or a USIS office. As Executive Assistant to USAID Mission Director Cap Dean at U.S. Embassy Pretoria since 1994, Kathryn Walsh says she learned long ago to always remain flexible and positive. "This is a very intense place, with lots of activity and public scrutiny," she said. "You have to remain focused on your work and never become unnerved by the constant interruptions and seemingly endless requests for information."

What's a typical day for a busy person like 50-year-old Walsh? "I don't know if there is one," she laughs. "Every day brings something new and different. It's interesting work, with a breadth of challenges. Let's just say it's never slow or boring."

As one of the largest USAID missions in the world, this post is also one of the most hectic. In 1995, 135 employees handled $187 million in U.S. assistance to South Africa. This country's new post-apartheid National Unity government of President Nelson Mandela has strong U.S. diplomatic and economic ties. The program is strongly oriented toward NGOs, with some 400 South African groups receiving U.S. funding through individual USAID grants in strategic areas of democracy and governance, education, health, economic policymaking, private-sector development and urban services. In 1994 President Clinton pledged $600 million in assistance to South Africa, of which $528 million is being administered over several years by USAID.

Walsh has worked for USAID for 20 years, handling a wide variety of assignments in a large number of differing office environments. She said the most important qualities of a Foreign Service Secretary are professionalism, confidentiality, high-quality work, and good management and teamwork skills. "It's particularly important to be good at relating to and working well with others, and to have a sense of humor," she pointed out. "Other pluses are perseverance and patience. You have to be able to see projects all the way through and make sure there are no loose ends."

After a nine-year stint as a Civil Servant for USAID in Washington, D.C., Walsh converted to the Foreign Service in 1985, following a two-month temporary assignment to Managua, Nicaragua, which hooked her on living overseas. "I came to realize that this is the kind of life I'd rather be living, where you can see the development in action, as opposed to just on paper," she said.

Her previous FS posts have included Yaounde, Cameroon, and Abidjan, Cote d'Ivoire. She attended Strayer Secretarial College, San Diego College of Business and Montgomery College. She was born in Washington, D.C., but considers Winter Park, Fla., her hometown. ■

CHAPTER 2

A DAY IN THE LIFE OF AN EMBASSY

By Nhien D. Le and Michelle R. Tatum

T he State Department, the conduit to which all embassy information flows, never sleeps. Through its 24-hour Operations Center, the eyes and ears of Washington are always open, watching and listening for whatever political, economic or natural development occurs in the world, be it military coup, terrorist attack, stock market crash or earthquake.

At each post, each key agency, such as State, USAID, USIS, and Defense — has a duty officer on call 24 hours a day. The rest of an embassy community is reachable by phone or radio. And the Ambassador, even if he or she is traveling, is always connected to the embassy and the State Department.

To better illustrate how an embassy works, key employees of six U.S. embassies in six very different parts of the world were asked to log their daily work activities for July 12, 1995. The result was a large sampling of events and daily activities, ranging from the important to the mundane, which were compressed into this chapter. The logs were coordinated by each post's Community Liaison Officer (CLO).

And, since many diplomatic initiatives can take months — sometimes years — to produce fruits from so much labor, each embassy provided its post's 10 top achievements of 1995, including contributions from representatives of USIS, USAID, FCS and FAS.

Participating embassies included U.S. Embassy Buenos Aires, Argentina; U.S. Embassy Dublin, Ireland; U.S. Embassy Amman, Jordan; U.S. Embassy Cairo, Egypt; U.S. Embassy Moscow, Russia and U.S. Embassy Canberra, Australia.

The embassies' top 10 achievements are impressive. They range from U.S. Embassy Buenos Aires' aggressive campaign against drug traffickers — culminating in the country's largest cocaine seizure in history — to U.S. Embassy Dublin's stunning behind-the-scenes success in helping to maintain an IRA ceasefire in Northern Ireland. But probably the most interesting deeds were performed at U.S. Embassy Moscow, which battled dozens of problems spawned by the end of the Cold War, from handling the huge growth of organized crime to convincing this ally of Serbia to accede to the West's policy on NATO peacekeeping in Bosnia.

For an easy reference guide to abbrieviations of embassy positions and acronyms and abbrieviations of U.S. government agencies used in this chapter, please refer to page 96. ■

Embassy Profiles

U.S. Embassy Buenos Aires, Argentina
Year opened: 1823
Number of U.S. government employees at embassy: 116
Immigrant visas issued in 1995: 1,162 (688 refused)
Tourist/business visas issued in 1995: 150,245 (2,824 refused)
In-country resident population of Americans: 25,000
No. of affiliates of U.S. companies/1995 U.S. direct investment: 121/$7.9 billion

U.S. Embassy Dublin, Ireland
Year opened: 1927
Number of U.S. government employees at embassy: 36
Immigrant visas issued in 1995: 1,435 (559 refused)
Tourist/business visas issued in 1995: 30,499 (2,607 refused)**
In-country resident population of Americans: 35,000
No. of affiliates of U.S. companies/1995 U.S. direct investment: 174/$11.1 billion

U.S. Embassy Cairo, Egypt
Year opened: 1922
Number of U.S. government employees at embassy: 483
Immigrant visas issued in 1995: 4,659 (2,268 refused)
Travel/business visas issued in 1995: 29,034 (16,955 refused)
In-country resident population of Americans: 11,868
No. of affiliates of U.S. companies/1995 U.S. direct investment: 46/$1.4 billion

U.S. Embassy Amman, Jordan
Year opened: Legation in 1949; embassy in 1952
Number of U.S. government employees at embassy: 117
Immigrant visas issued in 1995: 3,191 (4,208 refused)
Tourist/business visas issued in 1995: 14,448 (16,488 refused)
In-country population of Americans: 6,250
No. of affiliates of U.S. companies/1995 U.S. direct investment: 4/NA

U.S. Embassy Moscow, Russian Federation
Year opened: 1780
Number of U.S. government employees at embassy: 288
Immigrant visas issued in 1995: 6,371 (544 refused)
Tourist/business visas in 1995: 98,840 (38,412 refused)
In-country resident population of Americans: 6,360
No. of affiliates of U.S. companies/1995 U.S. direct investment: NA/$954 million

U.S. Embassy Canberra, Australia
Year opened: Legation in 1940; embassy in 1946
Number of U.S. government employees at embassy: 89
Immigrant visas issued in 1995: 0
Tourist/business visas issued in 1995: 10,094 (346 refused)
In-country resident population of Americans: 64,070
No. of affiliates of U.S. companies/1995 U.S. direct investment: 777/$65 billion

*Affiliates (more than 10 percent invested) are based on 1993 figures. **As of April 1995, visas no longer required for U.S. travel.

A Day in the Life of
U.S. Embassy Buenos Aires

Embassy positions featured at this embassy include the Political Officer (**POL**); the Agricultural Attaché (**AGR**) and the Administrative Officer (**ADMIN**).

(6:00) a.m. (Wednesday)　　　　　　**(4:00 a.m.** Washington, D.C., **Wednesday)**
Exercised on stationary bicycle for 45-minute workout, followed by shower and breakfast. **(ADMIN)**
Read newspapers at home. **(POL)**

(7:00) a.m.
Arose with 3-year-old, made breakfast and bathed her. **(POL)**
Read local newspaper over breakfast. **(AGR)**

(8:00) a.m.
Took daughter to school. **(POL)**
Left for hour-long train ride to office. **(AGR)**

(9:00) a.m.
Arrived at embassy; read cable traffic; scanned newspapers. **(AGR)**
Read cable traffic and newspapers. **(POL)**
Reviewed incoming e-mails and faxes. **(ADMIN)**

(10:00) a.m.
Had meeting with Foreign Ministry officials on who is going to the upcoming Fourth World Conference on Women. **(POL)**
Called USDA/W to announce changing wheat supply situation in this country. Due to nearly four months of drought conditions, the wheat harvest forecast dropped from a preliminary estimate of 11.5 MMT down to 8.5 MMT. Based on this reduced harvest, I alerted Washington to the possibility that by mid-1996, Argentina may be able to import wheat for the first time in many years. I also updated my monthly production and trade development figures of corn, sorghum, soybeans/products — meal and oil — and sunflower seed products. **(AGR)**

(11:00) a.m.
Drafted cable to D.C. on Foreign Ministry meeting and embassy's work on program for regional counterterrorism meeting set here in August. **(POL)**
Returned home to study FSN-retiree issue and to assist spouse in preparing for her first board meeting as commissary manager. **(ADMIN)**
Received call from economic officer in U.S. Embassy Asuncion to discuss use of credit guarantees for imports of U.S. cottonseed to Paraguay during fiscal 1996. **(AGR)**

(12:00) p.m.
Pick up daughter at nursery school and drop off at caregiver's house. **(POL)**
Lunch (ugh!) at embassy cafeteria. Bought package of Rolaids at embassy commissary. **(AGR)**

1:00 p.m.

Lunch with DOD officials to discuss upcoming Williamsburg, Va., conference, "Defense Ministers of America" to be attended next month by more than 30 ministers of Defense in the Southern Hemisphere. **(POL)**

Received call from Cotton Council International/DC concerning seminar here next month, hotel and reception arrangements, etc. Agreed to make a short presentation on Argentine cotton supply situation and requirements for obtaining import credits. **(AGR)**

2:00 p.m.

Picked up and read administrative reports. **(ADMIN)**

Updated computer databases for monthly Argentine grain and oilseeds/products exports. **(AGR)**

3:00 p.m.

Sent e-mail to RAMC-Mexico director regarding problems DEA personnel were having in receiving cost-of-living allowances; e-mailed State proposing Buenos Aires as test site for new program as substitute for FAAS. **(ADMIN)**

Met with DEA agents, who are writing a cable to Washington outlining funding priorities for the U.S. drug war in Argentina; returned to office to work on another cable. **(POL)**

Had lesson with Spanish tutor. **(AGR)**

4:00 p.m.

Received report on results of meeting of embassy's Commissary Board, which oversees post's mini-market where employees can buy limited stock of duty-free items, including groceries and liquor. Also discussed resignations from commissary club, for which embassy members pay an annual fee, because the board had decided to increase dues. Also learned that quarterly food shipment was coming in July and that $6,000 worth of State Department-embossed sweatshirts had been received. **(ADMIN)**

Conducted interview with local newspaper reporter on Argentine beef industry and prospects for fresh and frozen beef exports to the United States. As a major beef-producing country, Argentina has not been allowed to export fresh or frozen beef to the United States for almost 60 years, due to the existence of foot and mouth disease in this country, a highly contagious ailment. Now that Argentina has made great progress in eliminating this disease, the U.S government is expected to allow Argentine imports by late 1996, a move that would bring up to 20,000 metric tons of fresh and frozen beef annually into the States. **(AGR)**

5:00 p.m.

Met with embassy personnel on Foreign Ministry participation in the DOD ministerial meeting in Williamsburg, Va.

Spoke to SGSO regarding progress on telephone toll line, which will allow direct free voice communication with State and those U.S. embassies around world with similar systems. **(ADMIN)**

6:00 p.m.

Left embassy for home. **(ADMIN)**

Departed for home. **(POL)**

TOP 10 ACHIEVEMENTS OF 1995
U.S. EMBASSY BUENOS AIRES

■ The United States and Argentina have long been working together to combat narcotraffickers in the Southern Hemisphere. In summer, a two-year effort between the DEA and SIDE — the Argentine intelligence agency — culminated in the country's largest seizure in history: 1,000 kilograms of cocaine with a U.S. street value of $19 million. Nabbed in the arrest on a deserted airstrip near the capital were 11 South Americans. The embassy's senior officials, and the DEA have been working with Argentine officials to reform Argentine counternarcotics laws, which paid off when Congress approved the use of undercover police agents and authorized prosecutors to reduce sentences for defendants who cooperate in drug investigations.

■ Since an estimated $100 billion in drug money is laundered through Argentine banks every year, stemming the escalating flow has become a major joint initiative between the two governments. The Economic Section worked with the State, Treasury and Justice departments and their Argentine counterparts to organize the highly successful Summit of the Americas Ministerial on curbing money laundering, which was chaired by U.S. Treasury Secretary Robert Rubin. The meeting prompted firm commitments from the Argentine executive branch to strengthen the country's regulations and laws against money laundering in 1996.

■ The FCS office helped save millions of dollars for U.S. businesses this year. First, it convinced Argentina's government and the River Plate Commission to abide by the terms of a bid to dredge navigable channels in the Parana River and the River Plate, helping the Illinois firm of Great Lakes Dredge and Dock win a $144 million contract. FCS also convinced Argentine officials to reverse a decree, which had 2,000 tariff classifications prohibiting the importing of used parts for photocopy machines, facsimile machines and printers. Had it not been reversed, Xerox Co. would have been unable to fulfill its 25,000 service contracts in Argentina or to free $3 million in retooled Xerox parts that had been tied up in Argentine customs for six months.

■ Support for legal reform and broad judicial independence in Argentina have long been top embassy goals. Working with local legal experts and NGOs, the Political Section and USIS used $500 saved through the August 1995 shutdown of the USAID office to host a seminar focusing on three reform proposals, including one for a non-partisan judicial council to oversee the court system and the appointment of judges. The seminar so stimulated Argentine interest, its Congress is expected to pass legislation in 1996 mandating the creation of the council.

■ Many Argentines consider USIS's Lincoln Center as home to the country's best public library, with its wealth of up-to-date bilingual materials. Since opening in 1950 on Feb. 12, President Abraham Lincoln's birthday, it has served Argentines for more than 45 years. This year, 12,000 Argentines visited more than 72,000 times; took out more than 25,000 books, periodicals and audio and video tapes; and asked more than 30,000 reference questions. USIS Buenos Aires's fund-recovery plan, proposed in mid-1995 in the midst of Washington's cost-cutting measures, is expected to save up to $70,000 a year, 90 percent of the center's annual rent. Fees are now charged for annual library cards and time-consuming tasks such as CD Rom extract prints, database and other lengthy research searches, and photocopying. The plan has been so successful that it's being duplicated at other USIS libraries.

■ With the closing of the regional USAID office, hundreds of key Argentine NGOs working for government reform and civic education of voters — including the importance of public participation in government — have lost their major funding source. Overcoming initial Argentine resistance, the embassy's Political Section, USIS and FCS coordinated a breakfast meeting to introduce NGO executives to directors and members of the 450-member Argentine-American Chamber of Commerce. Both sides gained a mutual appreciation of the importance of civil education and government reform in the private sector. Impressed with the key role NGOs play in guaranteeing a fair and competitive business environment, several chamber members have now agreed to support some of the NGOs' key efforts.

■ Effective peacekeeping requires planning and practice. As part of the country's annual autumn military exercises, more than 230 soldiers from Argentina, Brazil, Paraguay, Uruguay and the United States gathered for two weeks to practice managing a joint peacekeeping command post. The exercise, termed United Forces, was coordinated by the Argentine military and the embassy's Defense Attaché office and Political Section, the U.S. Southern Command force and the Argentine Army. Observers from El Salvador, Honduras, Belize, Guatemala, Canada and the United Nations also participated. This was an important exercise for the Southern Hemisphere, allowing Argentina to demonstrate its hemispheric leadership in maintaining peace and strengthening security ties among Latin American nations.

■ More than 2,400 retired Americans in Argentina receive U.S. federal benefit checks from the SSA in Washington, which U.S. Embassy Buenos Aires mails to registered beneficiaries. Given Argentina's erratic mail service and bureaucratic bank system, the costs and headaches of implementing this program were often overwhelming. The Consular Section's pilot program to allow beneficiaries to collect their money through automatic teller machines as direct electronic transfers from SSA helped make that headache disappear. The 1,800 beneficiaries who have enrolled so far now save up to $20 a month in delivery and check-cashing fees. The program, which has also greatly reduced SSA costs for mailing and printing replacement checks, is expected to be adopted by many more embassies in 1996.

■ Argentina was one of the first countries to sign on to Project GLOBE (Global Learning and Observation to Benefit the Environment), Vice President Al Gore's worldwide environmental education initiative designed to engage adolescent students in learning about the environment. Data, such as temperature and rainfall in cities and towns worldwide, is transmitted to the United States and downloaded to the Internet. Yet without proper computer equipment at the three pilot high schools, Argentine students could neither transmit nor receive data. Since several U.S. computer manufacturers do business in Argentina, the embassy's Environment, Science and Technology Section organized a luncheon among U.S. company executives, which prompted Compaq Computer Co. to donate four computers to the project.

■ Embassy personnel from the Environment, Science and Technology Section and the Military Group coordinated a program to help 3,450 poor people in Tucuman province receive preventative medical and dental care during a summer Medical Readiness and Training Exercise. The program was run by the U.S. Army's 651st Hospital, a reserve unit; the Argentine Fifth Army Brigade; the Argentine Ministry of Health; Argentina's White Helmets, a humanitarian relief corps and by provincial authorities.

A DAY IN THE LIFE OF
U.S. EMBASSY DUBLIN

Embassy positions featured at this embassy include the Political/Economics Officer (**POL/ECON**) and the Consular Officer (**CONS**).

8:00 a.m. (**Wednesday**)   (**3:00 a.m.** Washington, D.C., **Wednesday**)
Arrived at embassy; read papers and telegraphic traffic. (**POL/ECON**)
Made first of several attempts to talk to someone in the Africa/Asia Division of the Irish Department of Foreign Affairs about a highly classified issue.

9:00 a.m.
Spoke with Ambassador's executive assistant about assignment for incoming intern.
Contacted Irish Fisheries Department about details of the U.S. Drift Net Fishing policy, which seeks to protect U.S. fishery interests by limiting the length of nets of foreign fishers in U.S. waters. (**POL/ECON**)
Compiled list of criminals for the month, which is clipped from newspaper reports by FSNs, and forwarded list to police contact, who will verify whether suspects were convicted. Once convicted, their names and birthdates are entered into the embassy's computerized lookout system. (**CONS**)

10:00 a.m.
Attended post's meetings of Visas Viper, an inter-agency program designed to identify the growing number of international terrorists and narcotraffickers. Every three months, all personnel at post meet to share information on potential or confirmed terrorists or narcotraffickers in Ireland; their names are sent to the computerized registries at State, Justice and Treasury. If confirmed as terrorists or narcotraffickers by Washington, the names are broadcast to U.S. posts around the world. At U.S. Embassy Dublin, the names are filed in Consular Section computers, so suspects will not be issued travel visas to the United States, if requested in Ireland. (**CONS**)

11:00 a.m.
Began drafting memo for Ambassador. (**POL/ECON**)

12:00 p.m.

1:00 p.m.
Lunch (**POL/ECON**)

2:00 p.m.
Held NIV interviews until 4 p.m. Went over today's 34 visa requests, which were either dropped off by applicants or received in the mail. Decided to issue 12 visas, interview further another five other candidates and to query 17 others for additional information to be sent via mail.
Wrote short cable on today's meeting of Visas Vipers group,
Wrote letter to local attorney defining an E-2 treaty investor visa, which, regulations say, "entitles an Irish non-immigrant to obtain a U.S. visa based on his capital investment

in a bona fide enterprise in the United States solely for the purpose of earning a living. The alien must intend to depart from the United States upon termination of E-2 status." **(CONS)**

③:00 p.m.

Spoke with Port Director of INS Preinspection Facility on variety of issues, including the problem of illegal alien nannies from Ireland who travel to the United States on tourist visas and stay on; and getting the appropriate visas for American teams of curling — a popular Irish sport that is a cross between ice hockey and bowling; and several problem cases.

Briefed him on Visas Viper meeting that he missed. **(CONS)**

④:00 p.m.

Answered follow-up questions from State Department on visit of George Mitchell, a former Democratic governor of Maine, who in November 1994 was named by the Irish and British governments to chair a three-person body to investigate the arms issue that has long stalled the Northern Ireland peace process.

The body, which also includes ex-Finnish premier Harri Holkeri and Canadian Defense Chief John de Chastelain, is expected to hold talks all this year to determine whether outlawed paramilitary groups must begin disarming before their political representatives can join negotiations on Northern Ireland's future. Britain is insisting that the Irish Republican Army (IRA) begin decommissioning its arms caches before its political wing, Sein Fein, can begin talks with the Ulster Unionists, the largest pro-Britain Protestant party and its main Catholic nationalistic rival, the Social Democratic and Labor Party. Also to be included in talks is the Ulster Defense Association, the largest loyalist armed group from Protestant areas of Northern Ireland, which stopped killing Catholics in October 1994 in response to the IRA's own ceasefire the previous month.

Representatives of the paramilitary IRA and the Ulster Defense Association said they will hold onto their weapons until they see if the multiparty negotiations progress. According to news sources, the IRA maintains an extensive stockpile of weapons, much of it supplied by Libya in the mid-1980s. The loyalist groups reportedly have only a few hundred guns. Many Protestants in Northern Ireland want continued British rule of that part of the island, but many Roman Catholics in Northern Ireland and the Republic of Ireland want the British out. Since the late 1960s, the IRA has killed more than 1,800 people; loyalist paramilitaries have killed about 900; and British soldiers and police have killed about 350. **(POL/ECON)**

Drafted and signed H-pass cables, which are messages on consular matters in response to U.S. legislators' questions. Wrote and mailed letters to inquiries on visa problem cases. Spoke with DCM concerning a key British official's son, who has requested a temporary work visa in the United States. Advised DCM that son should apply for visa in London, where he lives. **(CONS)**

⑤:00 p.m.

Attended short meeting with DCM to determine that he will make the demarche to the Irish Department of Foreign Affairs. Drummed up contributions to DCM's cable to Washington about the demarche. Afterwards, locked up and left embassy. **(POL/ECON)**

Took call from U.S. congressman's office concerning temporary worker visas. Explained they are approved in Washington and are only appropriate for summer jobs, such as for undergraduate students. **(CONS)**

⑥:00 p.m.

Went home. **(CONS, POL/ECON)**

Top 10 Achievements of 1995
U.S. Embassy Dublin

■ U.S. Embassy Dublin's crowning achievement was the successful coordination of President Clinton's Dec. 1-2 visit. In the eyes of the Irish government and its public, the event was a milestone occasion that recalled President John F. Kennedy's trip in 1963. Embassy personnel provided logistical support to some 800 White House personnel and press; served as a liaison with Irish officials in organizing events and meetings for the varied groups' schedules; and provided background and briefing papers used to prepare speeches of President Clinton and First Lady Hillary Rodham Clinton. The White House, the Irish government, and the U.S. and Irish press dubbed the visit a high-water mark in U.S.-Irish relations, particularly since its timing occurred at a critical stage in the Northern Ireland peace process. Clinton fondly remembered the trip as "the best two days of my life."

■ Major progress toward achieving peace in Northern Ireland was made in these 12 months, as the first year of quiet in decades echoed across the region. Remarkably, the August 1994 ceasefire of the outlawed terrorist group, the Irish Republican Army (IRA), held throughout the year. Ambassador Jean Kennedy Smith, who had helped broker the ceasefire, and her staff worked tirelessly — along with U.S. Embassy London and U.S. Consulate General Belfast (as well as U.S. Mission to the U.K.) — to speed up progress toward all-party negotiations on a lasting political settlement in the conflict. Buoyed by the long stretch of peace, President Clinton dropped the U.S. fundraising ban for Sinn Fein and invited its president, Gerry Adams, to the White House for St. Patrick's Day festivities. The Irish and British governments invited former Sen. George Mitchell, a Maine Democrat, to chair a key disarmament panel, giving the United States a direct role in the peace process.

■ At the embassy's initiative, the White House Conference on Trade and Investment was held in May in Washington, D.C. The event, which President Clinton addressed, was designed as an adjunct to the peace process in Northern Ireland by jumpstarting the region's stagnant economic climate through U.S. investment and development in Ireland, a perfect gateway to the large European Union market. To promote the event, U.S. Embassy Dublin hosted Secretary of Commerce Ron Brown, whose appearance helped draw top Irish business owners to Washington. Not only did the conference generate momentum for the peace process, but it sparked more than a dozen potential bilateral deals — and plans for a similar conference in Pittsburgh, Pa., in October 1996.

■ U.S. Embassy Dublin continued to press for increased U.S.-Irish trade, capturing the first-ever contract for a U.S. firm to supply communications equipment to the Irish military. Although several major U.S. companies announced joint ventures with local firms in the thriving Irish marketplace, embassy efforts focused on helping small- to medium-sized U.S. companies develop export marketing plans. For example, embassy personnel helped a California cookie company find an Irish partner to bake its products in Ireland, to be marketed locally and in the EU, and a U.S. dairy cooperative signed a supply agreement with an Irish-based dairy company.

■ Ireland has long been a favorite tourist spot and retirement locale for Americans, which makes for a hectic Consular Section even though only a relative handful lose their American passports or are jailed in Irish prisons every year. An estimated 35,000 American citizens live in Ireland, including a large expatriate retirement community. And another 200,000 American tourists visit every year, which easily makes Dublin one of Europe's most popular destinations for Americans.

■ Partly at U.S. Embassy Dublin's urging, Ireland has taken a more active role in preserving the peace in the former Yugoslavia and in sharing America's belief that maintaining European stability and protecting human rights are burdens to be shared. In 1995, Ireland committed 26 police officers to the International Police Task Force (IPTF) in Bosnia and provided, at U.N. request, a senior police official to head the IPTF.

■ Americans have long had a soft spot for the romantic Emerald Isle, which makes sense since the United States is home to 44 million Americans of Irish descent. Considering the deep cultural ties and affection between the two countries, U.S. Embassy Dublin was upset when the popular Fulbright scholar exchange program was threatened by 1995 budget cuts. Seeking to make the program financially self-sustaining, the embassy sponsored a golf tournament that raised thousands of dollars to fund the continued exchange of dozens of American and Irish academics in 1996. USIS, which handles the program, helped establish the first-ever Fulbright Alumni Association in Ireland, which will further widen the base of support for this key cultural program. The golf tournament was so successful, it's expected to become an annual fundraising event for the program.

■ Like many other posts, U.S. Embassy Dublin took Vice President Al Gore's Project Globe (Global Learning and Observation to Benefit the Environment) seriously, finding much enthusiasm among local educators and students. A June 22 bilateral agreement officially welcomed 18 schools across the republic to the worldwide program, designed to engage adolescents in learning about the environment by collecting local data, such as rainfall and temperature, and transmitting it via modem to the United States, where it's downloaded on the Internet.

■ U.S. Embassy Dublin saved millions of taxpayer dollars by cutting jobs and consolidating all embassy functions under one roof. Under downsizing imperatives, the post reduced State Department staff at post by 10 percent, cutting 11 Irish positions alone through a voluntary layoff package. The Political Section merged with the Economic Section, creating a Policy Management Office; the Consular Section returned to the main chancery, after years of leasing office space in a nearby building, a move expected to show $10 million in long-term savings.

■ In its ongoing effort to raise Irish consciousness on gender-equality issues, U.S. Embassy Dublin sponsored a number of well-attended women's events that culminated in an address by First Lady Hillary Clinton in December 1995. By providing a platform for women of Northern Ireland and the Republic of Ireland to share concerns about traditional views on their role in political and economic life on the island, U.S. Embassy Dublin is hoping to encourage women to feel empowered about making change in their lives.

A DAY IN THE LIFE OF
U.S. EMBASSY AMMAN

Embassy positions featured at this embassy include the Political Officer **(POL)**; the Economic/Commercial Officer **(ECON/COM)**; the USAID Mission Director **(USAID DIR)**; the USAID Deputy Mission Director **(USAID DEP)**; Public Affairs Officer **(PAO)**; the Cultural Affairs Officer **(CAO)**; and the Community Liaison Officer **(CLO)**.

6:00 a.m. (Wednesday)   **(10:00 p.m.** Washington, D.C., **Tuesday)**
Watched half-hour CNN World News report while dressing for work. **(CLO)**
Showered and shaved while listening to BBC World Service News on radio. **(POL)**

7:00 a.m.
Arrived at Ambassador's home for coffee with U.S. Deputy Assistant Secretary of State Toni Verstandig, visiting for Amman Economic Summit preparations. **(ECON/COM)**
As CNN droned in background, drafted memo on home computer to administration counselor for proposal decreasing living-quarter allowances as a cost-saving measure. **(POL)**

8:00 a.m.
Briefed by staff specialist on background of Princeton Tigertones, a university a capella group who performed in Petra yesterday. Prepared to return to embassy by 11:30 to prepare for two lunch-time public concerts at American Club. **(CAO)**
Read and responded to e-mails, including one to Ministry of Tourism staffer who says USAID is reluctant to finance Japanese-made computers to be installed at embassy offices. **(USAID DEP)**
Arrived at Allenby Bridge, the only overland route from Israel to Jordan, to assist with bridge-crossing formalities for Verstandig, who is escorted to Israel's West Bank. **(ECON/COM)**

9:00 a.m.
Arrived at embassy and read incoming cables. **(ECON/COM, CAO)**
Discussed arrangements for suddenly announced CODEL of Rep. Bill Richardson (D-N. M.), who is visiting to secure release in Baghdad of U.S. citizens William Barloon and David Daliberti. The men, who had been imprisoned for two months, had been jailed by Saddam Hussein when they inadvertently crossed the border from Kuwait into Iraq. **(POL)**
Held USAID Senior Staff meeting, in which main topic was whether to seek exemptions of operating expense cutbacks due to budget freeze. Morale is low. **(USAID DEP)**

10:00 a.m.
Drafted letter for Ambassador's signature inviting Jordanian companies to participate in OPIC Investment Mission to Jordan set for July 28-31. **(ECON/COM)**
Discussed language policy with boss. USIS will pay full tuition at American Language Center for embassy employees below Level 6 and half-tuition for spouses and dependent children. **(CAO)**

11:00 a.m.
Stopped by protocol office of the Jordanian Ministry of Foreign Affairs for impromptu meeting with Protocol Director Smir Masarwah to discuss arrangements for exchanging U.S.-Jordan extradition treaty ratifications, including details about ratification and logistics. **(POL)**

Met with members of Ministry of Finance and chairman of a local NGO to obtain ministry's approval to use program-generated funds to set up trust fund for local NGOs. **(USAID DEP)**

(12:00) p.m.
Picked up carryout kabobs and ate at desk, while going through overflowing in-box. **(USAID DEP)**

(1:00) p.m.
Gathered information on OPIC Mission and upcoming Pensions 2000 Investment Conference to be held in September here; distributed agenda to chairmen of five private-sector business organizations in Jordan. **(ECON/COM)**

Attended half-hour concert by the Tigertones at American Club which was well-received. **(CAO)**

(2:00) p.m.
Reviewed and cleared documentation for $70,000 grant to the Young Women's Christian Association to build small bakery in a poor area and employ a handful of locals. **(USAID DEP)**

Met with Ambassador to discuss press guidance for potentially sensitive U.S. visitor, scheduled to arrive tomorrow. He suggested that the visitor be shielded from the press, so he would not be tempted to respond to questions. **(PAO)**

Met Jordan Desk Officer Paul Thanos for lunch; we are joined by four Jordanian businessmen who work for U.S. companies in Jordan in the fields of manufacturing, bottling and finance. **(ECON/COM)**

(3:00) p.m.
Escorted four Jordanian TV crew members through security to the USIS auditorium for a live satellite roundtable program on marketing Jordanian products, sponsored by USIS. **(PAO)**

Attended WorldNet presentation, featuring U.S. investment counselor, who spoke via satellite with three Jordanian interviewers and an audience of 100 about how Jordan can better market its textiles, light industrial goods and agricultural exports. **(ECON/COM)**

(4:00) p.m.
Drafted memo for reorganization of USAID mission, to be sent to Washington. **(USAID DIR)**

Returned for last half hour of the Worldnet dialogue on marketing Jordanian products and stayed to talk briefly with departing guests. **(PAO)**

Summoned to ambassador's office for meeting on possibility of last-minute visit tomorrow by Special Middle East Coordinator Dennis Ross, who is in the region this week. **(POL)**

Made final catering arrangements for reception to be held at my home tonight. **(ECON/COM)**

(5:00) p.m.
Introduced Part 4 of American filmmaker Ken Burns' series on the U.S. civil war, which was attended by 20 Jordanians. **(CAO)**

Telephoned OPIC in D.C. to discuss upcoming visit to embassy. **(ECON/COM)**

(6:00) p.m.
Returned home, snacked, changed clothes, played tennis. **(USAID DEP)**

(7:00) p.m.
Showered, redressed for reception tonight, read newspaper. **(USAID DEP)**

Guests arrive for reception in honor of departing ECON/COM officer. **(ECON/COM)**

TOP 10 ACHIEVEMENTS OF 1995
U.S. EMBASSY AMMAN

■ During the three-day Middle East/North Africa Economic Summit in November, the embassy-operated American Business Center drew more than 1,000 visitors, including 165 U.S. business executives, 60 Israelis, 60 Palestinians and 180 Jordanians. The Country Team spent eight months preparing for the event, which was coordinated by the Economic Section, and was attended by two of Washington's top advocates of international business — Secretary of State Warren Christopher and Secretary of Commerce Ron Brown. This innovative people-to-people approach is one example of how U.S. Embassy Amman is helping to lay the foundation for regional networks of friends, family and business partners. Peace, U.S. diplomats are saying, can be profitable. The USIS staff, through its varied public affairs forums such as the televised WorldNet program, helped spread the word around the globe that the Middle East was open for business, in part by announcing a proposal to create a Middle East Development Bank.

■ Informal discussions between Economic Section FSOs and top Jordanian government officials helped encourage the passage — or repudiation — of two laws, a move that completely liberalized the country's investment climate. The Investment Promotion Law, passed in April, helped hike almost immediately foreign investment in the sectors of industry, agriculture, hotels, shipping and railroads. The law, which included regulations on income and sales taxes, also removed secondary restrictions on U.S. firms. More than a dozen U.S. firms — including MidAtlantic, CHA, Transglobal, Anadarko and Enron — have either signed or are planning to sign contracts for major projects in Jordan. This year, the government abolished the 11-year-old Trading With the Enemy Law, which had prevented Israelis from investing freely in Jordanian firms. Also contributing to the buoyant investment climate was Jordan's lifting of its 30-year-old boycott of products from Israel, which translates into greater opportunities for U.S. firms interested in regional business ventures.

■ U.S. Embassy Amman helped promote effective 1990 U.N. Security Council sanctions against Iraq — leveled after Iraq's Aug. 2 invasion of tiny Kuwait — by supporting the Jordanian government's strong actions, such as tightening border controls on goods moving from Jordan to Iraq, which accounts for the estimated $3 million of contraband confiscated so far this year.

■ Since Jordan is a strategic U.S. ally in the historically unstable Middle East, promoting cooperative military relationships between U.S. and Jordanian forces is a very important aspect of bilateral relations. This year, the embassy's Military Assistance Program (MAP) and the Defense Attaché Office (DAO) held 13 bilateral military exercises on Jordanian soil, the most comprehensive ever assembled in this country. Some 2,500 Jordanian soldiers participated. MAP and DAO coordinated the transfer of $7.7 million of surplus U.S. Defense Department ammunition and vehicles to the Jordanian military. The International Military Education and Training (IMET) program sent 168 Jordanian officers and civilians to the United States for various kinds of training, 105 for military exercises and 63 for classes on the importance of American democratic values.

■ USAID, in cooperation with Jordan's Ministry of Tourism and Antiquities and the American Center for Oriental Research, finally finished the four-year-long development of

Madaba Archaeological Park. The 1.25-acre park, partially funded with an $800,000 USAID grant, is the perfect showcase for hundreds of Jordan's most important mosaics, a well-preserved stretch of a street dating from the late Roman period and several reconstructed buildings believed to have been built in 560 AD. Madaba, a town of 35,000, was chosen because it is home to the country's most impressive mosaic, the first cartographic representation of the Holy Land. As a revitalized tourist destination, the town is expected to draw a record 200,000 visitors in 1996, dramatically more than the 144,000 counted this year.

■ Today, only 6 percent of new Jordanian mothers receive postpartum care, but USAID hopes to raise that figure to 60 percent by 1998, thanks to an $11 million program to establish postpartum centers in Jordanian hospitals. The nationwide project, which got under way this year, aims to establish and equip four postpartum centers to train up to 1,000 employees in health care and counseling skills, and eight postpartum outpatient centers for mothers and their newborns. In March, the country's first Comprehensive Postpartum Center for mothers and newborn infants opened at Al-Bashir Hospital, Amman's largest public hospital.

■ Jordan continued to be a strong U.S. ally in combatting terrorism in the region, particularly in its relationship with neighboring Syria, which remains on the State Department's list of nations that sponsor terrorism. U.S. Embassy Amman is a key player in antiterrorist activities by providing consultation and intelligence support to Jordanian officials. That help paid off with the foiling of the attempted bombing of several foreign-owned operations in the capital this year, culminating with the arrest of six members of the Islamic Renewal Movement.

■ For the first time in its 10-year struggle, the Bani Hamida Women's Weaving Project showed a profit this year, as the 1,200 women of this northern Bedouin tribe celebrated gross sales of $2.7 million, including $618,700 in exports to Europe and America. Leaders of the project, started in 1985 by the NGO Save the Children, helped convince weavers outside Madaba that they could sell their beautiful traditional weaving outside their village. The result? An increasingly sophisticated, self-sufficient women-owned and -operated industry. USAID gave its last grant — for $63,000 — this year; its previous grants included $326,000 in 1987 (through Save the Children) and $102,000 in 1990. Not only are the women able to maintain and celebrate their cultural heritage, but, as weavers, spinners, dyers, and loom setters, they are able to continue the centuries-old tradition of passing down skills from mother to daughter. Also, higher family funds have helped dramatically improve the health of the children of the village.

■ The Consular Section played a major role in setting up the August negotiations in Baghdad between Iraqi officials and U.S. Congressman Bill Richardson (D-N.M.), which helped free two imprisoned U.S. citizens, William Barloon and David Daliberti, who had inadvertently crossed the border from Kuwait into Iraq the previous week. Since America has no diplomatic relations with Iraq, this post helped arrange Richardson's visa to Iraq.

■ The Consular Section created a computerized list of in-country American citizens, the first of its kind at any U.S. embassy, which would be used as an emergency contact list in the event of a terrorist attack. Volunteer wardens would be able to contact via phone the estimated 6,250 American citizens to provide evacuation and other emergency information.

A DAY IN THE LIFE OF
U.S. EMBASSY CAIRO

Embassy positions featured at this embassy include the USAID Mission Deputy Director **(USAID DEP)**; the Community Liaison Officer **(CLO)**; the Medical Unit Nurse **(MED-NUR)**; and the Consular Officer **(CONS)**.

5:00 a.m. (Wednesday)   **(9:00 p.m.** Washington, D.C., **Tuesday)**
Walked my two dogs. **(USAID DEP)**

6:00 a.m.
Listened to radio news. **(CLO)**

7:00 a.m.
Left for office, where I opened office and checked my e-mail. **(USAID DEP)**
Arrived at embassy Health Unit. Checked day's patient schedule for physician. **(MED-NUR)**

8:00 a.m.
Began investigating American citizen's complaint that he had been prevented from leaving Egypt the previous night as he prepared to cross the Red Sea by boat, because he apparently was on some sort of Egyptian blacklist. **(CONS)**

9:00 a.m.
Met with American wife of U.S. citizen in prison, who is accused of being an Islamic extremist. Gave woman affidavits to allow her six U.S.-born children, who all came with her, to attend school in Cairo. **(CONS)**
Met with personnel of USAID/W Bureau of Policy and Program Coordination to discuss Population Council study of fertility determinants among Egyptian women, such as level of health and education, contraceptive availability, the role of religion and age at marriage. In Egypt, government and religious organizations are supportive of birth control; more than 40 percent of all women use contraceptives. **(USAID DEP)**
Treated patient with deep abrasion on her forehead. Attended staff meeting with Ambassador to propose cuts for fiscal 1996 budget in Medical Unit. **(MED-NUR)**

10:00 a.m.
Met with dual national citizen being held by Egyptian military for deserting group while in the United States for training. Though accused wanted another U.S. passport, he was told he would not be able to apply for another until the Egyptian military decided his case. **(CONS)**
Met again with DATT about recent deaths of two American active duty military personnel killed while on their honeymoon when the car they were riding in the Sinai hit a land mine. **(CONS)**
Returned to Medical Unit to treat patient with diarrhea. **(MED-NUR)**

11:00 a.m.
Responded to call from U.S. brother of American hospitalized in Egypt, who wanted details on embassy arrangements to fly him back to the United States today. Although the

patient's medical problem is severe enough to warrant immediate evacuation to the United States, the brother is not sure the flight is covered. He promised to call tomorrow. **(CONS)**

Treated patient with severe back pain. Gave another patient a tetanus booster shot. **(MED-NURS)**

(12:00) p.m.

Took a walk. **(USAID DEP)**

Interviewed 35-year-old American woman who wants to register Egyptian-born infant as American citizen. The case is suspicious because she says she came to Egypt just to give birth; her husband, who is reportedly in the United States, has not yet seen the baby. Since she is suspected of attempted adoption fraud, the registration of her child is denied. **(CONS)**

(1:00) p.m.

Called American woman who coordinated embassy's Volunteer Tax Assistance program last year to see if she would participate again next year. Also discussed program with area Americans who need help on their taxes. **(CONS)**

Briefed Washington-based FS nurse practitioner on meeting with Ambassador. **(MED-NUR)**

(2:00) p.m.

Contacted patient regarding recommended abdominal ultrasound. **(MED-NUR)**

Took call from front gate guard reporting an American woman needed assistance. She did not register with Egyptian police after arriving in Egypt a month ago, so she is now subject to a 28 LE ($9) fine before she can leave the country. She is protesting the fine, which the embassy can't help her negate, since her passport was stamped in English that all tourists must register with the police within seven days of arrival. **(CONS)**

(3:00) p.m.

Met with the father of a young jailed U.S. woman and the Consul General. Her father is considering hiring another lawyer, since new information has surfaced in her case and the first Egyptian lawyer was not considered aggressive enough in the Cairo court system. **(CONS)**

Prepared form for destruction of prescription drugs, which expire this month, at the embassy Medical Unit. Attended to two patients waiting in the Medical Unit, one of whom had a bleeding wound from falling in her house and the other of whom complained of abdominal pain, later diagnosed as a gastro-intestinal infection. **(MED-NUR)**

(4:00) p.m.

Had meeting with DOD attaché, at Washington's request, for information about two active-duty U.S. military soldiers accidentally killed on their honeymoon. It did not appear to be terrorism: As the couple was riding in the Sinai desert, their car hit a land mine. **(CONS)**

(5:00) p.m.

Left embassy. **(CLO)**

Had operator check my beeper; I'm on second call for Health Unit this week. Left embassy. **(MED-NUR)**

TOP 10 ACHIEVEMENTS OF 1995
U.S. EMBASSY CAIRO

■ The U.S.-Egyptian Partnership for Economic Growth and Development, one of three major worldwide initiatives spearheaded by Vice President Al Gore in 1993, aims to deepen U.S.-Egyptian economic relations by promoting trade, investment and technology transfer and job creation in Egypt. Word of the country's increasing openness to U.S. business is spreading fast. Pepsico opened a $50 million production facility in Cairo in 1995, creating 50 new jobs. FCS FSOs helped McDonald's and Chili's open franchises and aided the Erie, Pa.-based General Electric Co. crack the locomotive market with $30 million in sales. Ford Motor Co. was feted at an Ambassador's reception in May, celebrating the auto giant's return after a 10-year hiatus. First-month sales were $10 million. Egypt attracted U.S. portfolio investors, who this year purchased 30 percent of new privatized companies. And the liberalization of the banking and financial sector helped American Express and Citicorp achieve record-high profits this year and drew U.S.-based financial leaders Merrill Lynch and Solomon Brothers into the marketplace.

■ Egypt continues to be a key broker in promoting the peace process in the Middle East, specifically between Israel and the Palestinian Liberation Organization (PLO) and between Israel and Syria. Though it's been two years since PLO leader Yasser Arafat and Israeli Prime Minister Yitzhak Rabin signed the Declaration of Principles in 1993, embassy diplomats have worked tirelessly behind the scenes to negotiate three detailed agreements stimulated by the declaration. Those accords, signed this year, call for the withdrawal of Israeli forces from the Gaza Strip and the West Bank and the transfer of civil authority of those two areas to the Palestinian government. Embassy employees aided as interpreters, note takers, messengers and informal advisers to both delegations, and transmitted regular reports to Washington.

■ Since Egypt is a strategic military location in the Middle East, multinational military cooperation has long been an important aspect of its bilateral relationship with the United States. In November, U.S. Embassy Cairo helped Egypt coordinate a massive land, sea and air military exercise, nicknamed "Bright Star '95," which recreated the concept of an international coalition, such as the one formed for Desert Storm in 1991. Some 51,000 troops from four countries carried out the exercise on land northwest of Cairo and on the north coast, at sea in the Mediterranean and in various points of Egyptian airspace. The group included 21,000 U.S. soldiers and 30,000 from the United Arab Emirates, the United Kingdom and Germany.

■ U.S. software companies have long complained of rampant piracy of their products in Egypt, but U.S. Embassy Cairo helped engineer an arrangement that has become a regional successful model of private-public sector cooperation in the region. Working with local industry leaders, the embassy encouraged the Egyptian government to draft, pass and implement the most far-reaching anti-piracy legislation in the Middle East. Not only did the embassy organize an effective lobby of U.S. software companies to press their message to Egyptian officials, but it also sent Egyptian police and judges for U.S.-based training on how to enforce the new law. The cooperative effort also led to a multi-million dollar U.S. investment to develop Arabic software for a Cairo-based regional distribution company and prompted the Motion Picture Association of America to open a regional office in the capital to work with Egyptian officials in protecting its clients.

■ After nearly three months of tough negotiations, Egypt — considered a moderate Arab state — persuaded Libya — considered a radical Arab state — to cede its place on the U.N. Security Council — a key U.S. foreign policy goal this year. U.S. diplomats believe that Libya, which was in the second year of a rotating two-year spot on the 15-member board, had upset the balance of power on Middle East and terrorism issues. The council's permanent members, who have veto power, include the United States, China, France, Russia and the United Kingdom. Five new temporary members are added each year for two-year terms. The council's mandate is to maintain international peace and security.

■ Egypt is believed to be a main source and target of concentrated global terrorist activity, so improving the security and intelligence network is an important bilateral goal. The Consular Section sponsored a drive to hike the number of resident American volunteers for its warden program, designed as a security network to alert other resident Americans quickly in the event of a terrorist attack or to pass on tips about potential terrorist acts. More than 2,000 additional wardens were added to the 2,500-member network. An estimated 11,900 Americans live in Egypt.

■ Reforming the country's antiquated, inefficient and backlogged civil justice system is one of the Egyptian government's most important goals, so U.S. Embassy Cairo has added its help. Various USIS- and USAID-sponsored programs helped bring U.S. and Egyptian legal experts together to discuss ways to improve the legal climate, which officials say is conducive not only to increased justice for the average Egyptian citizen, but also for local business owners and foreign investors. The Institute for the Study and Development of Legal Systems signed on as the U.S. partner to teach case management and alternative dispute resolution techniques. Plans for 1996 include drafting new court legislation and training programs for legal professionals. The embassy's efforts will culminate in a two-day Ministry of Justice conference set for Jan. 3-4 in Cairo.

■ USAID, whose Cairo office is the largest in the world, has long been a strong proponent of Egyptian programs to improve Egyptians' standard of living through reduced population growth levels and access to better health care. It seems to be paying off. In the last decade, population growth has declined dramatically in this country, from 3.3 percent to 2.2 percent. USAID's Infant and Child Survival Program contributed to a 43 percent drop in infant mortality between 1980-95 and an astounding 65 percent drop in child mortality rates during this same period. And in 1995, diarrhea was eliminated as a principal cause of death among children, thanks to a long-term USAID oral rehydration program. A record 90 percent of children are now covered through USAID's expanded immunization program.

■ Security, which has been a long-term major concern at U.S. Embassy Cairo, was enhanced this year by several embassy-led initiatives, including a $35 million security upgrade with state-of-the art metal-detection machines at each entrance and motion-sensor devices. And in a new program Diplomatic Security expects to offer annually, more than 500 Egyptians learned to deter terrorist attacks in public spaces at a one-week seminar conducted by U.S. security experts.

■ The Political Section held several intensive training programs with the People's Assembly for the country's 25 newly elected legislators. The programs provided basic information on the role of democracy, constituency building and consensus building in the legislative process. One key aspect was a day-long seminar on alternative dispute resolution.

A Day in the Life of
U.S. Embassy Moscow

Embassy positions featured at this embassy include the Economic Counselor (ECON); the Agricultural Officer (**AGR**); the Consular Officer (**CONS**); the Political Officer (**POL**); and the Personnel Secretary (**PERS SECY**).

7:00 a.m. (**Wednesday**)   (**11:00 p.m.** Washington, D.C., **Tuesday**)
Walked the dogs. (**AGR**)
Groaned through step aerobics class at embassy gym. (**CONS**)
Watched CNN while eating breakfast. (**POL**)

8:00 a.m.
Drove to Embassy. Dropped by Consular Section to report actions taken as Duty Officer on midnight to 8 a.m. night shift. Reported an interesting call during shift, in which two Russian professors requested expedited visa service because they had hoped to stop in the United States before going to a conference in Mexico, but had been denied entry onto the plane in Moscow. They were able to get reservations on the plane for tomorrow, but the embassy would still have to speed up duo's U.S. visa applications. This morning, Consular Section promised visas would be waiting for the two when they arrived that morning. (**AGR**)
Arrived at embassy, and stopped by CLO's coffee to welcome five new embassy employees. (**PERS SECY**)

9:00 a.m.
Called the Plant Quarantine Service — also known as the Russian State Commission for Plant Protection and Quarantine, an official Russian ministry — to discuss proposed trip by U.S. officials to study whether fresh U.S. fruits and vegetables can be exported to Russia without disease or pests spreading to Russian plants. (**AGR**)
Informed consular employees of Consul General's decision to limit walk-in visa applicants to 400 people today, due to backlog caused by computer breakdown yesterday. Handed over $50,000 in consular fee collections from yesterday's visas. Afterwards, three junior officers and I conducted visa interviews with more than 100 people; more than 70 were issued visas. (**CONS**)

10:00 a.m.
Wrote EPA-required letters to ministries of Environment and Agriculture giving notice that U.S. exporters shipped box of pesticides to Russia, which was not registered for use in the U.S. (**AGR**)

11:00 a.m.
Received fax and call from U.S. Consulate St. Petersburg. Import certificates from a U.S. container of food, which Russian Customs claimed were forgeries, had been sent to the Embassy. Confirmed they were forgeries and faxed copies to Washington for USDA. Although case has not been settled, document's forger is expected to lose his shipment — and the cash — from the anticipated sale. (**AGR**)
Returned to embassy to set up meeting tomorrow with editor of major local newspaper to talk about Caspian Sea demarcation and oil pipeline routes from Azerbaijan. U.S. officials are seeking to esure that U.S. oil companies have equal opportunity in the Caspian oil fields. (**POL**)

12:00 p.m.

Lunched with CLO-recommended nanny for my soon-to-be-born child. **(CONS)**

1:00 p.m.

Gave background briefing on privatization, enterprise restructuring and defense conversion in Russian Federation to correspondent of *Wall Street Journal*. **(ECON)**

Lunched with colleague. Upon return, answered numerous questions from calls and walk-ins on promotions, embassy visa procedures and third-country exit visas. **(PERS SECY)**

2:00 p.m.

Reviewed cable from U.S. Embassy Almaty, which says Kazakstan is interested in receiving U.S. credits for oilseed imports, under a USAID-financed program for U.S. exports. USDA is aggressively promoting export of U.S. products and commodities, including soybeans. Made recommendation to Agricultural Counselor that U.S. message to Kazakstan government indicate USDA is prepared to offer $15 million credit to purchase U.S. soybeans. **(AGR)**

Cleared with Legal Attaché's office draft telegram on visa fraud connected to Russian organized crime figure being investigated by FBI. Understandably, this is a common task: This office is requested to send the FBI lists of names or addresses appearing on invitations or sponsorships to the United States, which is required to verify the legitimacy of the business or person. This FBI check has prompted the arrest of many people on visa fraud. **(CONS)**

Updated Emergency Notification Warden System and solicited Americans to volunteer as wardens in telephoning embassy personnel and families in the event of an emergency. **(PERS SECY)**

3:00 p.m.

Went with FSN on visits to Russian psychiatric hospital to visit two American citizens with gifts of fresh fruits, shampoo and soap. Both appeared physically well, although they expressed concern about quality of meals. Spoke with their doctors about their nutrition and the eyeglass repair of one of the women. Took notes so as to send letter to women's families in the United States. **(CONS)**

4:00 p.m.

Met with a potential U.S. cotton importer, who pointed out that imports processed in Russian Federation and re-exported as clothing to that country are allowed to enter VAT-free. **(AGR)**

Returned phone calls from embassy's Economic Section and U.S. Agriculture Department in D.C. regarding status of pending visa cases. Also answered calls from seven Americans, including one from a U.S. legislator, asking about visa refusals to visit the Russian Federation. **(CONS)**

5:00 p.m.

Briefed incoming Economic Officer on USDA programs in Russia. **(AGR)**

Called NFATC regarding proposed project with Russian Diplomatic Academy that would allow U.S. diplomats to study the Russian language at its Moscow campus. **(POL)**

6:00 p.m.

Workday ends in flurry of phone calls; Washington's now awake and wants information. **(AGR)**

Ran end-of-day report on the $50,000 collected in consular fees. **(CONS)**

7:00 p.m.

Met friends for an evening sauna at local Russian banya. **(AGR)**

Attended new play, "Hell's Garden" with Russian Ministry of Foreign Affairs contact. **(CONS)**

TOP 10 ACHIEVEMENTS OF 1995
U.S. EMBASSY MOSCOW

■ Since the end of the Cold War, strengthening political and security ties between the United States and the Russian Federation has been one of the foremost goals in U.S. foreign policy. In accomplishing that end, U.S. Embassy Moscow promoted political reform and stability; organized thousands of scientific, cultural, parliamentary, business and political exchanges between the two countries; handled 130 inspections of Russian military sites under various international arms control agreements; and ensured the safe elimination or removal of thousands of Russian nuclear weapons from Ukraine and Belarus.

■ Opening avenues for American products and investment in Russia spelled huge success for this post this year. Diplomats from the Commercial Section had their busiest travel season ever, logging tens of thousands of miles as they promoted the idea of stronger bilateral economic ties to bankers, businessmen, economists, farmers, legislators, traders, oil company owners, miners and ordinary citizens across Russia. The collapse of the Soviet Union in 1991 helped usher in a market economy that prompted 250 U.S. firms to open offices this year alone. FCS officers opened six more American Business Centers this year, bringing to 10 those in Russia: in Chelyabinsk, Khabarovsk, Niznevartovsk, Nizhniy Novgorod, St. Petersburg, Vladivostok, Volgograd, Yekaterinburg and Yuzhno-Sakalinsk. More than 1,000 U.S.-based businesses used the centers to set up temporary offices, do market research, locate local distributors and bid on local projects. A key sticking point in the U.S.-Russian business relationship was resolved this year, thanks to tough negotiating by U.S. diplomats: The Yeltsin government finally agreed to U.S. patents and trademarks protection laws.

■ The escalation of organized crime, drug trafficking, money laundering and white-collar crime in Russia in recent years has prompted U.S. Embassy Moscow to make law enforcement cooperation and security training a top priority. Its Law Enforcement section, including the FBI's Legal Attaché office, organized 60 Russian-language seminars for 1,500 law enforcement professionals at sites in Russia, the United States and Hungary. Joint cooperation between Russian and American law enforcement specialists paid off this year with a number of stunning successes in solving crimes against Americans. In only three days, Diplomatic Security agents helped free a 43-year-old U.S. businessman kidnapped by a group affiliated with Chechen organized crime. And, after a one-year investigation, a 2-year-old American child kidnapped as an infant from his mother's Los Angeles house was rescued unharmed in Cyprus and returned home. The kidnapper was extradited to the United States to stand trial. In addition, the Legal Attaché Office worked with Russian, Israeli and British authorities to crack a 10-member Russian computer crime ring that had moved $10.4 million from New York bank accounts to fake ones in other countries; all but $400,000 was recovered.

■ Russian participation in ending the Bosnian civil war was critical to the eight months of negotiations that culminated in the Dayton Peace Accords in November. U.S. diplomats in Moscow helped convince Russia to deploy a full brigade of Russian soldiers in the NATO peacekeeping force in Bosnia. Russia, which is sympathetic to the Serbs, had previously opposed even the use of NATO air power in the region.

■ Consular Section FSOs had an extraordinarily busy year, helping American parents adopt more than 1,400 children from Russia and other former Soviet republics. Consular officers also spent uncountable numbers of hours explaining to 2,000-plus prospective American parents and U.S. adoption agencies a March law that halted international adoptions for nine months and required Russian families to have the first chance to adopt local orphans. American interest, however, remained so intense and adoption requests so numerous that when the law was rescinded in December, the Consular Section began gearing up for 1996, a year that promises a record number of American adoptions of Russian orphans.

■ FAS efforts helped hike U.S. exports this year to Russia to $700 million of consumer-ready foods, including meat, poultry, fruit and snack foods, making the United States the largest overseas poultry supplier for Russia. In June, when poultry exports were threatened with higher tariffs, the Embassy worked with Russian officials to have the hike eliminated. Under the Cochran Fellowship Program, FAS sponsored 15 delegations with a total of 280 Russian public officials and academics for short-term U.S.-based training in agricultural policy, economic reform, business management and agricultural extension. Other groups of private business owners visited U.S. agricultural trade shows in Chicago, New York, Atlanta and San Diego; FAS-sponsored trade shows in Moscow and St. Petersburg drew 90 U.S. food exporters.

■ The foundation of a well-regulated — and potentially huge — capital market was laid, thanks to a $73 million USAID grant. Building on critical USAID support for the ongoing privatization program, a Commission on Securities and the Capital Market was established; private organizations, such as share registries and a NASDAQ-clone electronic trading system, were developed; and the Duma agreed to consider legislation that would make it illegal to break the new securities rules. In 1995, foreign investment through the stock market averaged $500 million a month and 120 new companies were formed.

■ USAID programs supporting democracy and emerging economies realized solid success, even though program funding levels had plummeted to $300 million from a 1994 high of $1 billion. The programs supported training to independent TV and radio journalists to improve news programming; political and economic debates among the growing number of NGOs, which will be this country's next governing class; and independent election monitoring that helped ensure fair and free Duma elections in December.

■ Russia's new political openness provided USIS with an unprecedented opportunity to expand contacts in this historically closed society. Exchange programs allowed 7,500 Russians to travel to the United States, including 300 political and community leaders, through the International Visitors and Fulbright programs. Dozens of Americans received grants for study and research on subjects and in regions previously closed to Westerners. While much in Russia remains uncertain, these exchanges help build a cadre of Russians with first-hand knowledge of America and an ever-expanding network of Russian-American contacts.

■ Another major achievement was coordinating the semi-annual meeting of the Gore-Chernomyrdin Commission (GCC) in March, presided over by U.S. Vice President Al Gore and Russian Prime Minister Victor Chernomyrdin. Embassy officers provide the research and administrative support for GCC, established in 1993 to encourage bilateral trade, environment, science and technology projects.

A Day in the Life of
U.S. Embassy Canberra

Embassy positions featured at this embassy include the Defense Attaché (**DATT**); the Consular Officer (**CONS**); the Agricultural Officer (**AGR**); the Economic Officer (**ECON**); and the Commercial Officer (**COM**).

7:00 a.m. (**Wednesday**)   (**2:00 p.m.** Washington, D.C., **Tuesday**)
Listened to local TV and radio news while dressing for work. (**DATT, CONS**)
Left for embassy. (**CONS, AGR, DATT**)

8:00 a.m.
Arrived at American-Australia Chamber of Commerce for meeting of International Trade Committee to develop prospective activities for potential Asia-Pacific Chamber of Commerce. (**COM**)
Discussed actions of the day with supervisor and reviewed schedule for visit of head of U.S. Veterans of Foreign Wars and his adjunct, Gen. Larry Stevens, who were visiting to understand U.S. diplomatic and military activities in the area and report their findings to VFW members. (**DATT**)
Telephoned FCS personnel in Sydney and Melbourne to coordinate reply to a Washington telegram on U.S. businesses interested in the Australian market. (**ECON**)

9:00 a.m.
Told woman her company would need to apply for a petition with both the U.S. Department of Labor and the U.S. Immigration and Naturalization Service, and that petition, if approved, would be sent to the applicant. If the Consular Officer finds her unqualified for the job, the petition may be rejected.

10:00 a.m.
Left embassy for airport with driver to meet U.S. plane scheduled to land at 10:45 a.m. with an American VIP, who is scheduled to lay a wreath at the national Vietnam Memorial and to speak at the Returned Servicemen's League. (**DATT**)
Advised U.S. permanent resident regarding requirement for U.S. passport for her infant, also a U.S. citizen, and the potential consequences of her attempting to enter the United States without a passport for the child. (**CONS**)
Called on president of local beef association about exporting beef to the United States, who said local ranchers were concerned about overly stringent U.S. pest control regulations. (**ECON**)
Joined meeting with Ambassador to provide views on Australian competitiveness in exporting oil, minerals and clothing (lamb and sheep wool) and importing U.S. cars, airplanes, textiles and hi-tech equipment. (**COM**)

11:00 a.m.
Meet with Ambassador to discuss Australia's veterans affairs, including the United States' reestablishing of diplomatic relations with Vietnam. Australia has never broken diplomatic relations with Vietnam. (**DATT**)

Responded to request from FCS Sydney for economic data to be printed in "Business Down Under," a guide for U.S. businesspeople interested in operating in Australia. **(ECON)**

Took call from Australian with offer of U.S. job; explained distinction between immigrant visa, which would allow him to permanently live and work in U.S., and temporary work permit, granted to foreigners working for U.S.-based firms. Permit does not provide immigration status. **(CONS)**

12:00 p.m.

Finished morning's 57 visa requests. Counted applications and confirmed we issued 39 visas and denied 18. This denial percentage is higher than usual; in an average year, only 150 of 10,000 requests are denied. Met husband and other staffers for lunch at Embassy. **(CONS)**

Lunched with Australian-American Chamber of Commerce directors, and discussed Australia's economic policy and complaints about double U.S.-Australian taxation of resident expatriates. **(ECON)**

Attended luncheon hosted by New South Wales Chamber of Manufacturers. **(COM)**

1:00 p.m.

Went to Australian War Memorial to lay wreath and tour memorial grounds during week-long festivities commemorating the 50th anniversary of the end of World War II. **(DATT)**

2:00 p.m.

Drafted letter to U.S. sister of American killed in scuba diving accident, advising her of status of U.S. investigation of the accident. Embassy to assist in obtaining coroner's death certificate. Embassy assists with return of body, but needs to ensure that cost of returning body is paid by family. **(CONS)**

Met with political counselor to help draft embassy's response to State's recommended budget cuts, which would slash the number of FSOs by one-third and FSNs by one-fourth. **(ECON)**

3:00 p.m.

Sought information, at DEA's request, on American drug trafficker due to be released from a Canberra prison next month. Passed message on to DEA. **(CONS)**

4:00 p.m.

Entered visa-check system on computer to confirm all names of visa applicants were not previously refused for a visa and did not have a history of illegal activity, such as visa fraud, or had terrorist or drugtrafficking connections. While waiting, called Justice Department to discuss pending extradition case for two Australians, one accused of child molestation and the other of drug trafficking. The Australian-U.S. extradition treaty allows for the return of Australians accused of committing U.S. crimes. **(CONS)**

5:00 p.m.

Took call from CNN reporter on economic consequences of five-year drought, which has intensified since March 1994. The drought has devastated Australia's farm economy. Winter crop production in fiscal 1994 dropped 50 percent from the previous year. **(ECON)**

6:00 p.m.

Reviewed today's events at embassy and confirmed tomorrow's schedule. **(DATT)**

Before leaving Embassy, made sure office was secured and all passports in safe. **(CONS)**

TOP 10 ACHIEVEMENTS OF 1995
U.S. EMBASSY CANBERRA

■ Australia has become more important to the United States in the last decade, as the Land Down Under became the southern anchor of the U.S. network of treaty alliances and a bulk-head of stability in the Asian-Pacific region. Strong U.S.-Australia security ties remain the No. 1 priority at U.S. Embassy Canberra. The alliance was formalized after World War II with the signing of the ANZUS security pact among Australia, New Zealand and the United States, although New Zealand reduced its participation in the mid-1980s. With the 1992 closing of the U.S. bases in the Philippines, U.S. military personnel are stationed at only a few Pacific bases: Japan, the Republic of Korea, Guam — and, of course, Australia. U.S. Embassy Canberra helps maintain the delicate balance of regional security by encouraging Australia's active participation in the annual meetings of the ASEAN regional forum, a subgroup of Association of Southeast Asian Nations (ASEAN), including Brunei, Indonesia, Malaysia, Phillippines, Thailand, Singapore and Vietnam, plus 14 other countries and an EU represen-tative, which consider regional security issues. The two allies this year began talks to expand the joint spy satellite base at Pine Gap in Australia's outback and to build another ground station at the site, part of Washington's proposed space-based ballistic missile early warning system.

■ FAS recorded some stunning successes this year, as the section battled its Australian coun-terparts to resolve some of the most bitter of bilateral conflicts over agricultural products. After more than a year of intense negotiations among members of the trade bloc APEC (Asia Pacific Economic Cooperation), the U.S. diplomats successfully ensured that agricultural products would be included in the free-trade agreement, which calls for the dropping of tariffs among the developed nations of the United States, Australia, Japan, Canada, New Zealand and Singapore by 2010. APEC's developing nations would drop their tariffs by 2020. Agriculture is the world's most heavily government-subsidized sector, so its exports have complicated many trade bloc negotiations. U.S. Embassy Canberra FSOs also made great progress toward lifting the decades-long Australian ban on U.S. salmon and chicken part exports, a potentially huge export market for U.S. farmers closed for decades due to Australians' fear of transmitted ani-mal diseases.

■ In trade circles around the world, Australia's claim to fame has long been as the country with whom the United States has its largest trade surplus. In 1995, that gap slightly widened again, with two-way trade totalling $15 billion and the United States enjoying a $9 billion favorable balance of trade. Australia officials worked with embassy FSOs this year to achieve agreement on a blueprint for increased foreign exports to the region in the next decade.

■ Privatization of government-owned industry continued at a brisk pace this year, as for-eign companies — predominantly American — purchased a handful of public utilities, pre-dominantly in the electrical power sector. That was no surprise to the Aussies, for whom the United States' $65 billion investment has made it the No. 1 foreign investor in Australia. By the way, Australia is the No. 8 investor in the United States.

■ Australia has quickly become one of the most attractive narcotics transshipment points for heroin from Southeast Asia to the United States, and for South American cocaine destined for

Southeast Asia. Working closely with the DEA, Australian officials established a get-tough drug policy that culminated this year in the seizure of 460 kilograms of amphetamines, the largest of its kind in the country's history. Not only do U.S. embassy and Australian officials share drug-trafficking intelligence, but they trade techniques on combatting laundering of drug funds and the eradicating of cannabis crops.

■ An estimated 424,000 Australians visited the United States this year, coughing up $2.5 billion for the U.S. tourism industry. And another 475,000 Americans traveled to Australia in 1995 to check out the kangaroos and visit the outback. So when the Consular Section this year succeeded in eliminating the need for two-way travel visas for Australian and American citizens, the section's workload dropped by more than one-third. Geographically as large as the United States and host to four time zones, Australia has a population of only 18.3 million — as many as the Americans who live in the state of Pennsylvania. The wanderlust for Australia must be pretty strong: It's a 13-hour plane trip from Los Angeles — and 20 hours from Washington.

■ The Political Section worked hard to prepare for what promises to be one of the most interesting elections in modern Australian history, as the Labor party, in power for 13 years, readied to face off against the Coalition Party in spring 1996 elections. Although the embassy is not permitted to support either party, it has had historically close ties with both groups. USIS did its share to bring understanding of both political systems by sponsoring Republican and Democratic staffers from Capitol Hill and their counterparts from the Canberra parties on a two-week mutual exchange program.

■ If your country harbored the world's longest coral reef, as Australia does, you, too, might seek the world community's help in protecting this fragile ecological miracle. U.S. Embassy Canberra's Environmental Office helped Australian officials stay abreast of new technology and World Bank grants to protect the 1,250-mile stretch of coral reefs and islands along the country's eastern shore, the Great Barrier Reef. Embassy help was also instrumental in kicking off the first meeting of the International Coral Reef Initiative, held in July in the Philippines, which featured Vice President Al Gore as the keynote speaker. The Australians are expected to take the helm next year as head of the 15-member group.

■ Although U.S. Embassy Canberra doesn't do much publicly to promote better treatment of the country's 50,000 Aborigines and 150,000 half-Aborigines, it has long supported the government's efforts to ease racial tension between its majority white population and this tiny black minority. Concentrated in several preserves in the Northern Territory, the Aborigines are not only economically disadvantaged, but representing only 1 percent of the country's population, have little political clout. The embassy's Political Section monitors discrimination against the group for Washington's annual Report on Human Rights.

■ Long known as one of the world's most activist environmentalists, Australia is often at the forefront of worldwide initiatives to protect the environment. As part of the U.S.-Australia Memorandum of Environmental Understanding signed last year at U.S. Embassy Canberra, a high-ranking official of the Australian counterpart of the Environmental Protection Agency (EPA), the highest U.S. authority on environmental laws, is spending this year at its Washington, D.C., headquarters to research how to better enforce Australian environmental laws.

CHAPTER 3

THE FSO
IN ACTION

CONTRIBUTIONS TO THE
FOREIGN SERVICE AND U.S. DIPLOMACY

By Laura Ngo

FSOs and Foreign Service employees around the globe work hard to carry out America's diplomatic mission abroad, but there is no typical experience. Unlike elected U.S. representatives or the Secretary of State, FSOs can work quietly behind the scenes — or quite openly, as do USIS officers sending America's message abroad — to achieve diplomatic and economic goals through skillful and subtle diplomacy that may take years to yield success. As representatives of the U.S. government on the ground, FSOs make the first contacts with a host country's leaders, intellectuals, business people, journalists and youth. And, as the following personal stories illustrate, it is often those personal contacts that help resolve some of the thorniest challenges facing U.S. foreign policymakers.

Individual members of the Foreign Service have made singular contributions to the profession and to American interests abroad. But it's dangerous over there: Many of these first-person accounts are filled with drama, heroism and intrigue, war, peace, terrorism, kidnapping and murder.

Mid-level FSO Les Hickman recalls witnessing the opening shots of the Persian Gulf War from his vantage point on the Kuwaiti-Iraq border. Former Ambassador L. Bruce Laingen recalls the horrors as a hostage in Iran from 1979-81. Former USAID Mission Director Ronald E. Venezia describes helping victims of the 1991 earthquake in Costa Rica. Former USIS Press Attache Bruce Byers remembers the grisly 1979 assassination of Ambassador Adolph "Spike" Dubs in Afghanistan, and ex-PAO Susan Crais Hovanec reminds America that war is still hell, as she reports on this decade's most contentious conflict — in Croatia.

Other pieces chronicle the difference a single FSO can make, such as F. A. "Tex" Harris' account of blowing the whistle on the Argentine military during the "Dirty War," or of former FSO Charles Johnson, whose population control work in Indonesia helped a USAID program that reduced births by a dramatic 39 percent over 27 years. And some stories capture the realities of Foreign Service life, such as Senior FSO Phyllis E. Oakley's description of life as a woman in State's old boys' network of the late '50s, or the belief of Mary Ryan, Assistant Secretary of State for Consular Affairs, that the Consular Officer is the most unappreciated of FSOs.

However, all these tales echo a common theme. Each Foreign Service employee's unique combination of interpersonal and diplomatic skills, mixed with more than just a dash of courage, have contributed to the collective goal of serving America and Americans overseas.

These are the true stories of the U.S. Foreign Service in action. ∎

THE VOLUNTARY HOSTAGES
KUWAIT, 1990

By Barbara Bodine

On Aug. 9, 1990, after illegally annexing Kuwait, Iraqi President Saddam Hussein issued one of his many ultimata: All embassies were to close by noon, Aug. 24, 1990, or become consulates — or he and his military would lay siege to the compounds. No government agreed to the terms or the deadline, although all embassies evacuated their dependents and non-essential personnel. Eight members of U.S. Embassy Kuwait City agreed to stay beyond the deadline, even though many more than eight volunteered. Why face a siege of indeterminate length but clear conditions? For two reasons that are the essence of diplomatic representation abroad: to show the flag, in this case literally, and to serve and protect the American private citizens trapped in Kuwait and subject to Iraqi abuse.

After the invasion, the embassy served as a sanctuary to any American citizen seeking refuge from the Iraqis; at one point it housed nearly 200 people, a third of whom were private U.S. citizens. Most other embassies did the same. The Japanese, at great risk to themselves, also took in almost 20 U.S. embassy staffers for 10 days.

With no phones, no access to the American community and more than enough armed guards about, we were not at all sure how we could help Americans trapped in Kuwait, but there was no question that to leave behind U.S. citizens, either on compound or in Kuwait, would have been not only unprofessional but immoral. So, the American Embassy stayed opened for business-not-as-usual for 137 days, until Dec. 13, 1990.

And, in the end, our decision to stay paid off. Against the odds, reasonable hope and logic, we accomplished our "Mission Impossible." Over the course of 13 chartered flights out of Kuwait, we evacuated every American citizen who wished to leave, the nationals of more than 30 other countries otherwise unable to get out, and, ultimately, the 400-plus American men in deep hiding and the 19 on the compound with us. With our mission accomplished, we could close the compound and go home — leaving the American flag still flying over Kuwait City.

Barbara Bodine was Deputy Chief of Mission in Kuwait City, Kuwait, in 1989-90. Bodine, who joined the Foreign Service in 1971, has served in Hong Kong; Bangkok, Thailand; Tunis, Tunisia; and Baghdad, Iraq.

NURTURING A FRAGILE DEMOCRACY
HONDURAS, 1981

By Jack R. Binns

On Nov. 29, 1981, the people of Honduras elected a new government that took office on Jan. 27, 1982, ending 17 years of military rule. Since then, Honduras has successfully held three free, democratic elections and orderly transfers of powers. And on two of these occasions, the governing party handed the reins of government to opposition parties — an excellent performance nearly anywhere in Latin America, but in Honduras, it was unprecedented.

But it was not easy getting there. The 1981 elections, in fact, were nearly blocked by the Honduran military. In early October of that year, the armed forces' high command, with a single dissenting officer, decided to oust the transition government of Gen. Policarpo Paz Garcia, cancel elections and resume direct rule. This plan failed, largely due to a thoughtful U.S. policy effectively implemented by the hard work of many at U.S. Embassy Tegucigalpa.

Our overriding policy priority was simple: To utilize all available means to ensure the successful transition to democratic, constitutional government, beginning with fair elections in November 1981 and ending with installation of a freely elected government in January 1982. Attaining this objective, moreover, was of critical importance to the entire U.S. regional policy in Central America; indeed, it was the keystone of our policy arch. Democracy, we believed, was the most effective defense against replication of radical regimes, such as the Sandinista government in Nicaragua that held power from 1979-90.

Even before I arrived in Tegucigalpa in October 1980, we knew that key senior Honduran officers had begun to question their earlier decision to turn over the presidency to political parties. We also knew that the vast majority of Honduran people, and nearly all of their institutions, such as the media and independent political parties, supported the transition from military rule to democracy. In the past, however, the military had repeatedly shown its readiness to sacrifice the country's national welfare to advance its own narrow interests. We feared this might happen again, especially if the military's fear about the designs and intentions of the Sandinistas grew, as in fact it did.

Our strategy for preserving the transition process fell into shape quickly. It was to be a classic public diplomacy effort, designed to leave no one in Honduras doubting that the United States was firmly and unequivocally backing the return of democracy. At the same time, in meetings with every sector of society, we Americans would emphasize and reiterate that continued U.S. economic and security assistance would be contingent upon completion of the transition process.

Through the efforts of an outstanding Public Affairs Officer, Cresencio Arcos, who would later become U.S. Ambassador to Honduras, we were able to enlist the support of the owners and editors of nearly all major media outlets in the country. We also persuaded most of our important American visitors — congressional, executive branch and military — to reiterate this message at home.

With few notable exceptions, our efforts fell on fallow ground. The Honduran exceptions were, in addition to the military and a small number of its allies: the leaders of the National Party and the extreme left. Sen. Jesse Helms (R-N.C.) and his staff were American exceptions: They kept in close touch with events in Honduras, visited several times, but did not once speak out in support of the transition process.

The National Party leader, Ricardo Zuniga, an effective and devious political operative, feared — correctly — that he would not win the elections. To derail the elections, he worked closely with those military leaders who did not wish to cede power to a civilian government. He also manipulated the visiting Helms delegations, successfully — but erroneously — convincing its members that the Liberal Party, which ultimately won the elections, was closely aligned with the Sandinista movement and represented a grave threat to U.S. interests. Opposition from the far left was based on the realization that elections constituted a barrier to revolutionary change, a la Nicaragua.

The military's midnight decision to foreclose on the elections was made at a special meeting of senior commanders on Oct. 10, 1981. The dissenting commander of the Air Force, Col. Walter Lopez, now Vice President of Honduras, argued that a coup could lead to increased popular unrest and was folly in view of the U.S. government's strong support for democratic elections. His was a lone voice.

Once the decision was made, Col. Lopez went immediately to his headquarters, placed the Honduran Air Force on alert and armed all aircraft. He then began contacting lower-level army unit commanders, whom he believed supported him, to advise them of the decision and request their support — and he got it. Col. Lopez also contacted the Liberal Party presidential candidate, Roberto Suazo Cordova, alerting him to the impending coup, urging that he go into hiding and requesting that he pass this information on to me, which was done.

By the time I assembled key members of the embassy's Country Team, the coup threat was imploding. Army unit commanders simply refused to obey the high command. Subsequently, most of those who opposed the coup — military, political, private sector — credited the U.S. government policy and its implementation by the embassy for maintaining popular support for a democratic transition. I regard this as my most important contribution to the conduct of U.S. foreign policy, a feeling broadly shared by all those who served in the mission at that time. We made a difference.

Jack R. Binns, who retired from the Foreign Service in 1986, was U.S. ambassador to Honduras in 1980-81. In his 25-year career, he served in Guatemala City, Guatemala; La Paz, Bolivia; San Salvador, El Salvador; London, England; Madrid, Spain; and as DCM in San Jose, Costa Rica.

ASSASSINATION OF AN AMBASSADOR
AFGHANISTAN, 1979

By Bruce K. Byers

Valentine's Day 1979 dawned clear and cold for members of U.S. Embassy Kabul. And, as we would see soon enough, it would be a day like no other in our careers. As Press Attache for USIS, I had worked with PAO Roger Lydon and Ambassador Adolph "Spike" Dubs since my arrival in June 1978 to present official U.S. policy to the various ministries of the Marxist-led Afghan government and to help American journalists seeking access to Afghan officials.

Shortly after 8 that morning, Ambassador Dubs, 56, a career FSO, was on his way to the embassy in his bullet-proof vehicle, when men dressed as Afghan police stopped it near the USIS compound. Using a ruse, the armed men persuaded the driver to open his window, forced their way into the car and drove the Ambassador to Kabul Hotel in the city's center, where they took him hostage in an upper-floor room. The U.S. Embassy driver returned to the embassy to announce the kidnapping.

A stand-off ensued until shortly after noon. Just as U.S. officials believed they had persuaded Afghan Interior Ministry officials not to storm the room, at about 12:30 p.m. a gunshot was heard. Police in the hotel corridor and on rooftops across the street opened up a fusillade into the room that lasted more than a minute. Afterward, silence. Later, Ambassador Dubs was found dead, his body ridden with bullets. None of us at the embassy knew what this event portended or whether it was the beginning of a coup against the government of President Mohammed Tariki, the nominal head of the Khalq Party, a pro-Moscow Marxist organization competing with the rival Parcham organization for control of the Afghan government.

Earlier that morning, when Lydon returned to USIS with news of the Ambassador's kidnapping, I decided to make an audio record of embassy radio transmissions, using a two-way radio on the embassy's frequency to monitor and tape transmissions among Kabul Hotel colleagues, and staff at the embassy and in vehicles moving between these locations and the Interior Ministry, where the Afghan government was trying to manage the crisis. Transmission quality varied, but they helped embassy security officers construct a chronology of events for analysis in Washington.

In the hours and days that followed, I worked with Chargé d'Affaires Bruce Amstutz, Political Counselor Bruce Flatin, Public Affairs Counselor Roger Lydon and other embassy colleagues in preparing responses to journalists from the United States, Europe, South Asia and elsewhere. Within 24 hours after the killing, dozens of western journalists had poured into the city and wanted to know what impact the killing would have on U.S.-Afghan relations. I was impressed at the intensity of interest in America about our crisis in Kabul.

It would have been easy for us to hint at links between Soviet KGB and Afghan Interior Ministry officials, but we had to remain absolutely disciplined about information released to the media and the public. The truth was that we had very few hard facts. Any public speculation by embassy officials could have precipitated more dangerous developments in a country whose Marxist-led government was already worried about its survival. The chief responsibility of our embassy was to safeguard the lives of the more than 4,000 Americans living in the country and, especially, those in Kabul.

The kidnapping and murder of Ambassador Dubs remained a mystery for years. We did not know who the hostage takers were, even though three had been taken alive, or what organization they represented, and apparently neither did the Afghan government. The kidnappers had been demanding the release of prisoners who the Minister of Interior claimed were not even in the country.

Through the traumatic days and weeks after the killing, the embassy staff and the international community pulled together. We Americans demonstrated that our mission would not be deterred from its responsibilities to represent our government and our nation in this geostrategically important country. In a simple ceremony in the embassy compound we later honored our fallen ambassador, remembered as a U.S. Marine who had survived the bloody battles of the Pacific in World War II.

As in similar events in other U.S. diplomatic missions — Khartoum, Beirut and Islamabad, to name three — FSOs and their families stood firm in the face of terror and violence and represented the best ideals and values our country offers in the oft dangerous field of international diplomacy. For those who served in Kabul, this is our tribute to "Spike" Dubs.

Bruce K. Byers was USIS Press Attaché at U.S. Embassy Kabul from 1978-79. Byers, who joined the Foreign Service in 1971, also has served in Tehran, Iran; Bombay, India; Vienna, Austria; Bonn, Germany; Washington, D.C.; and Warsaw, Poland.

ON THE BRINK OF A TRADE WAR
(JAPAN, 1994-95)

By Keith Curtis

One doesn't need to look far to find articles about a Japan "at the crossroads," which note the myriad changes in Japanese society ranging from young people no longer wearing kimonos to political systems that invite public debate over elections. The years

I spent in Japan from 1991-95 were a time of real political change. The 40-year rule of the Liberal Democratic Party was broken in 1994, which prompted the appointment of four Prime Ministers in 18 months.

With the 50th anniversary of the end of World War II approaching in 1994, these political changes created new tension in the U.S.-Japan relationship, for many years considered a key diplomatic tie to American leaders. The Japanese economy was slowing due to bad debt from failed real estate speculation in downtown Tokyo; Japanese business leaders were screaming for greater deregulation; and for the first time, Japan was importing more televisions than it exported.

It was no accident then that the liberalization process began with the breaking of the bond between business and bureaucracy, one of three linked constituencies, with the third one politics. New laws largely eliminated the surreptitious cash flow from business owners to politicians, and in the resulting political paralysis, the government bureaucrats — never known in Japan for their affinity to change — gained greater influence over the political process.

Amidst this change, U.S. Embassy Tokyo was clearly focused on tracking and analyzing political changes, on maintaining the strong U.S.-Japan alliance and on pursuing the further opening of Japanese markets to U.S. products. This third goal had become dramatically more important since the Cold War ended, and with the increasing U.S. trade deficit with Japan, which was now at $60 billion. In 1993, the Clinton administration declared a results-oriented trade policy based on previously successful agreements in the semiconductor and auto parts industries.

From fall 1994 through spring 1995, U.S. diplomats in Tokyo and Washington worked endless hours with officials of the newly strengthened Japanese bureaucracy, reaching 15 different agreements in sectors ranging from medical technology to apples. Finally, the focus turned to the hardest nut to crack — auto trade, representing almost 60 percent of the U.S. trade deficit between the two countries. I was responsible for the auto-sector portfolio in the embassy's Commercial Section, spending most of my time counseling U.S. business on marketing strategies in the Japanese market, but being inevitably drawn into negotiations over auto imports and exports.

After a year of political wrangles and crises, by 1994, Japan and the United States had arrived at the brink of a major trade war. The United States filed an unfair trade complaint against Japan in the World Trade Court, where the Japanese, in turn, bought a case against the United States, seeking to disarm U.S. trade leverage and to embarrass America in the court of public opinion.

On June 29, 1995, the day before sanctions were set to begin, both teams' principal trade negotiators met in Geneva. Late that afternoon in Tokyo, a major Japanese auto company called me to arrange a meeting with its CEO and U.S. Ambassador Walter Mondale to avert sanctions. After a series of late-night meetings and phone calls, the Ambassador, his staff and I were able to convince the Japan Automobile Manufacturers Association that the largest five Japanese auto companies — Toyota, Honda, Nissan, Mitsubishi and Mazda — should publicly support the U.S. proposal that Japan encourage much wider U.S. access to its markets. At 5 a.m. that day, the White House called to request documents confirming the companies' agreement to seek an increase in Japanese purchases of U.S. car parts by $9 billion over three years, moving from $19 billion to $28 billion. For the last 25 years, 40 million Japanese cars had been exported to the United States; during that same period, only 400,000 American cars had been allowed on the Japanese market.

Even though it took many months of tough negotiations and one long night on the brink, it was worth it to break down Japan's long-standing trade barriers to American auto products and to avoid the most severe trade war in the two allies' history.

Keith Curtis has been an FSO with the Foreign Commercial Service (FCS) since 1990, after 10 years of working in the International Telecommunications Division of McDonnell Douglas Corp.

SURVIVING TERRORISM
LEBANON, 1983

By Anne Dammarell

USAID Program Officer Tish Butler recalled her first reaction to the April 18, 1983 bombing of the U.S. Embassy in Beirut that killed 66, summing up many FSOs' first thoughts during the tragedy: "I remember feeling a strong sense of responsibility to try to pull the group together and to decide what to do to make sure everybody was O.K. I was scared, since I didn't know where the bomb had come from."

Instinctively, Butler wanted to rescue the injured. She was not alone. Other surviving colleagues felt the same way. Despite the danger — we were all aware of the terrorist technique of setting off a second bomb to target rescue workers — they searched for the wounded amid the debris. Several survivors would later mention that they first secured their filing cabinets before finding a way out of the crushed building.

When the embassy was hit, I had been in Beirut for nearly all of a three-year tour — my first overseas assignment as an FSO — and I had but one week left before leaving for my next assignment in Colombo, Sri Lanka. One of only two survivors in the decimated embassy lunch room, I spent the rest of 1983 and the following two summers in and out of hospitals, mending 19 fractures. Determined to "get back on the horse," I had been happy to start the delayed tour in Colombo in January 1984. But it was there that the anxiety attacks became stronger, worsening as the months progressed. When two USAID contractors were kidnapped, my anxiety level zoomed upward. Was my life on the line again? It would take me another five years until I could say that I had truly recovered from the bombing.

For a master's degree thesis at Georgetown University, I interviewed the FSOs who survived the 1983 attack to determine what effect the assault had had on our lives. What I found was a group of courageous individuals with a "can-do" mindset, who revealed a deep sense of loyalty to their government, their jobs and their colleagues. Many continue to trust the Foreign Service with their lives. U.S. Embassy Beirut Political Officer Ryan Crocker captured the sense of commitment this way: "I think it is very important when you come out of something like this to have a sense that what you did was important and that you are not some battered survivor. You had a mission."

Terrorism has become the preferred — perhaps the only — method by which impotent nations conduct war against powerful world rulers. In recent years, terrorists — with quick-strike flexibility and reliance upon theatrical symbolism — have zeroed in on the U.S. diplomatic community. They've also upped the ante, from capturing an entire embassy of ready-made hostages in Iran in 1979 to kidnapping and killing a U.S. ambassador in Kabul that same year. Those incidents were followed by bombings of the U.S. Embassy in Lebanon in 1983 and again in 1984.

Since terrorists view diplomats as combat personnel, embassy security has increased and mission staff may find it increasingly difficult to be as open with the foreign community as had been possible previously. Embassy as fortress is now no mere metaphor. In some countries, it is a reality.

Anne Dammarell, who was USAID General Development Officer from 1980-83 in Beirut, retired from the Foreign Service in 1988. In her 23-year career, she also served in Colombo, Sri Lanka, and Washington, D.C.

TALKING TO MUGABE
MOZAMBIQUE, 1975

By Willard DePree

In 1975 the United States had to decide how to deal with the newly independent government of Mozambique. Alarmed by the close relations of President Samora Machel and his ruling party, Frelimo, with the Soviet Union, China and Cuba, and his harsh criticism and openly expressed suspicions of the United States, some believed America should not open an embassy, saying we had little to gain. Until this point, only a U.S. Consulate had been open and Congress had even legislated a ban on development assistance to that country. Other U.S. diplomats, however, thought it too early to write off Mozambique.

Bordering on Rhodesia and South Africa, Mozambique was bound to be a key player in the future of racially plagued South Africa. It was in the United States' interest to maintain open lines of communications, and if it was too much to expect Mozambique's cooperation, maybe it would be possible to keep its officials from poisoning U.S. initiatives in the area.

The small mission in Maputo, to which I was the first Ambassador, was of the second persuasion: We thought there was a role for diplomacy. However, it would not be an easy job. The first year the Mozambican government kept the mission at arm's length and subjected personnel to a great deal of petty harassment. Officials had no interest in consulting with the United States; President Machel even turned down Secretary of State Henry Kissinger's offer to visit Maputo. Yet there were a few bright spots. The government harbored a hard core of Communists, but they were not dominant; Machel and the majority in the Cabinet were more pragmatists than idealogues. Disillusionment with communist aid and with state management of the economy was setting in. The war in Rhodesia was spilling across the border and seriously damaging the economy: Mozambique desperately needed a settlement in Rhodesia.

Meanwhile, the U.S. mission sought every opportunity to dispel Mozambican suspicions of the United States and to demonstrate that there was an alternative to relying on the Communists. When floods and drought struck, the United States was quick to respond with relief assistance; when Mozambique proved incapable of feeding its growing refugee population, the U.S. shipped in food aid. We at the mission kept Machel abreast of our continuing efforts to achieve settlements in Rhodesia and Namibia.

With developments inside and outside Mozambique working to our advantage, Machel's reservation about cooperation with the West changed. Not only did he begin to receive the British and U.S. negotiating teams, but he eventually saw himself as working in tandem with us. Suspicious — with some reason — that Rhodesian Prime Minister Ian Smith and the British might be seeking to exclude Robert Mugabe and the Zimbabwe African National Union (ZANU) from a post-independence government in Rhodesia, he urged us and the British to bring Mugabe and ZANU more fully into negotiations. He saw Mugabe as the key, and the U.S. mission shared this view.

A settlement, however, eluded the British. Finally, in December 1979, Prime Minister Thatcher invited all the parties to a London conference. After several days of discussions, a settlement seemed near. But Mugabe balked. With delegations making reservations to return home, it looked as if the conference would fail. At this point, I received instructions on behalf of President Jimmy Carter to appeal to President Machel to intervene with Mugabe. Time was of the essence. Fortunately, after four years in Maputo, I had developed a good working relationship with the president and he agreed to see me. I assured him the United States would continue to work closely with the British to ensure a free and fair election. If he and Mugabe were convinced that they would win the backing of the majority in the election, then they had won. Would he weigh in with Mugabe to conclude a settlement? After some thought, Machel looked me in the eye and said, "Yes, you can tell President Carter I will talk to Mugabe." And he did. Later the British told us that had it not been for Machel's intervention, there would have been no settlement and no peace in Rhodesia.

The U.S. government's patience and perseverance and our diplomatic presence on the ground in Maputo made a difference.

Willard DePree was U.S. Ambassador to Mozambique from 1976-80. Before retiring from the Foreign Service in 1993, he also served in Cairo, Egypt; Nicosia, Cyprus; Accra, Ghana; Freetown, Sierra Leone; in Dhaka, Bangladesh, as Ambassador; and in Washington, D.C., as Director of Management Operations at the State Department.

A FRAMEWORK FOR DEMOCRACY
NIGERIA, 1975-79

By Donald B. Easum

It is sometimes tempting to describe the importance of a USIS office by focusing on the numbers: how many articles were placed in the local press, how many exchange program visitors were sent to the United States, or how many American specialists interacted with how many local leaders. For such statistics to be truly meaningful, however, one must go beyond the numbers and identify the ways in which such activities contribute to definable U.S. interests. Let me illustrate with the following retrospective salute to the splendid performance of our USIS mission in Lagos during 1975-79, a critical period in the U.S.-Nigerian relationship.

I arrived in Lagos in April 1975, inheriting a dedicated embassy/USIS team from my predecessor, Ambassador John Reinhardt. But no combination of U.S. mission talents could have predicted or prevented the challenge that would confront us in Africa's most important country after South Africa.

Gen. Yakubu Gowon was in his fifth year as Nigerian head of state, having orchestrated a remarkable reconciliation between the warring factions in the fratricidal Biafran war. But Gowon's popularity was rapidly evaporating as his government proved incapable of controlling an oil boom economy spinning wildly out of control. His regime's lack of managerial grasp was spectacularly illustrated by hundreds of cargo ships — one-eighth of the world's merchant fleet, it was said — that lay anchored offshore of Lagos, prey to mutiny, pillage and scuttling.

Gowon then reneged on his promise to schedule a return to civilian rule. This and the general chaos of governance provoked his military brethren to move against him in a bloodless coup on July 29, 1975. The new head of state, Gen. Murtala Muhammed, promptly announced a timetable for returning to civilian rule by Oct. 1, 1979, the 19th anniversary of Nigerian independence.

With vigor and imagination, USIS Director Jack Hedges and his staff seized the opportunity to assist the move toward democracy through an array of activities. But within four months, our best intentions had collided with geopolitical reality. South African armored units moved into southern Angola in late September 1975, in support of Jonas Savimbi and his UNITA forces. Convinced that the United States had secretly encouraged the invasion, Nigeria abandoned its policy of neutrality and opted for full support, including major financial and military aid, for the Marxist-supported MPLA regime in Luanda. Not surprisingly, the United States was soon being portrayed in the Nigerian press as an ally of a racist South African regime.

In early January 1976, relations worsened when the Nigerian government released to the press a personal letter to Gen. Murtala from President Gerald Ford, which appeared to Nigerians a patronizing attempt to legitimize the South African invasion. The Lagos newspapers printed the letter under an extra-large headline, "FORD'S LETTER IS FATUOUS INSULT TO BLACK AFRICA." Angry crowds demonstrated outside the U.S. Embassy and USIS offices. We put a hold on plans for unwrapping the USIS democratization assistance package.

And then came the events of Feb. 13, 1976. Murtala was assassinated by Army Major Buka Dimka, a trigger man under instruction from the ambitious Minister of Defense Gen. Iliya Bissala. The Lagos press immediately charged the United States and the United Kingdom with complicity in the plot against a regime that had been rapidly making a mark on African diplomacy with its aggressive espousal of the liberation struggle in southern Africa. The U.K. High Commission offices and our embassy were again besieged by demonstrators, this time doing greater damage to the U.S. chancery than the first protest six weeks earlier. The U.K. High Commissioner was expelled by the Nigerian government. Prominent U.S. businessmen were arrested and detained for days without reason or notification. My house was picketed by angry students. Threatening letters arrived through the mail or were mysteriously delivered by messengers.

Now this is not the sort of environment in which USIS programs would be expected to prosper. But we reasoned that as long as Gen. Olusegun Obasanjo, Murtala's successor, demonstrated his determination to carry out democratic elections, it was very much in the U.S. interest to support and shape the pre-vote process. We started unwrapping the package, and the USIS Lagos team swung into action, now headed by Public Affairs Officer Art Lewis, assisted by his deputy, Ed Noel, Cultural Affairs Officer Sam Thomsen and Information Officer Robert Krill.

USIS contributed to Nigeria's decision to replace its British-style parliamentary system with a U.S.-style presidential system by delivering extensive resource materials on the U.S Constitution and system of government to the military government's Constitutional Drafting Committee; by distributing related material to Nigeria's 19 daily newspapers, five TV stations and 14 radio stations; by coordinating on-the-job training with the Associated Press for the new government-sponsored News Agency of Nigeria; and by providing U.S. International Visitor Program grants to selected journalists, government ministry officials and potential candidates for political office to witness U.S. government and court systems in action.

USIS gets the lion's share of credit for the dramatic turn-around in Nigerian attitudes toward the United States during this four-year period, highlighted by President Jimmy Carter's historic visit to Lagos in March 1978 and capped by the inauguration of President Shehu Shagari after multiparty elections in October 1979. Shagari was reelected four years later. Although ousted by the Nigerian military in December 1983, the constitutional processes by which he took office and under which he served remain alive in the memories of hundreds of thousands of Nigerians today.

Donald B. Easum was U.S. Ambassador to Nigeria from 1975-79. Before retiring from the Foreign Service in 1980, he also served in Managua, Nicaragua; Jakarta, Indonesia; Dakar, Senegal; Niamey, Niger; Ouagadougou, Upper Volta; and as Assistant Secretary of State for African Affairs. Robert Krill, Information Officer from 1977-79 in Lagos, collaborated in the preparation of this essay.

FIGHTING THE 'DIRTY WAR'
ARGENTINA, 1977

By F. A. "Tex" Harris

In October 1977, as a mid-level officer starting my second overseas tour, I was asked by the U.S. Embassy's Political Counselor Bill Hallman in Buenos Aires, Argentina, to take on responsibilities for a new area of diplomatic activity — human rights. I agreed, on the condition that the strict restrictions on uninvited visitors to the U.S. Embassy be relaxed to allow me to interview everyone complaining about human rights abuses. The embassy worried that this would draw a flood of victims' relatives to the mission, but I felt strongly that the job could not be done unless I met directly with the families who felt they had been wronged. People flooded in by the scores each day, reporting facts on the "disappearance" of relatives or loved ones.

We at the embassy, who had lived through months of threats and the terrible murder of a USIA officer at a branch post, had reported the "disappearances," in the context of the "Dirty War" between left-wing terrorists and the right-wing militia. My daily interviews, which I kept on 5x8 cards that eventually totalled 15,000, soon painted a clear picture of a massive, coherent, military effort to exterminate Argentine citizens.

At first, my telling of this story to the U.S. government was applauded by embassy personnel, from Ambassador Raul Castro on down. Then the practical implications of the new Carter human rights policy became clear. Actions of the U.S. government towards Argentina were no longer to be based on Ambassador Castro's recommendations, but on the behavior of the Argentine government, as documented in our human rights reporting. A classic battle began with the front office trying to put a more favorable "spin" on my human rights reporting. As it became more difficult to report the full details of human rights abuses in diplomatic telegrams, I used airgrams, memoranda of conversations and official-informal letters — none of which required front-office clearance — to send the facts to Washington by classified air pouch. My major confrontation with senior embassy officials came when one of my letters, which had been copied to Ambassador Castro, was withdrawn from the diplomatic pouch, and I was requested not to send it. The information in that letter resulted in the cancellation of a multi-million-dollar U.S. government loan guarantee to a major American corporation to provide turbine technology to a front corporation owned by the Argentine Navy.

As a young FSO, it's tough to fight with the Ambassador over policy issues. I took a stand based on the need to get the full facts and all points of view back to Washington, and knew my performance evaluation might suffer. I was almost fired for insubordination, but after an independent review, I was given only a formal warning. In 1993, with the benefit of historical hindsight after two decades, the State Department conferred upon me for my actions its highest recognition — the Distinguished Honor Award.

Outside the embassy in 1977, things were much easier. As an American diplomat, my information about the military junta's "disappearance" program authenticated and provided a context for the multitude of personal reports that journalists from around the world received when they came to Argentina. And my extra tall (6' 7") official American diplomatic presence and open support for the Mothers of the Plaza de Mayo and other human rights groups gave a clear signal that the American government and its people abhorred what was happening in Argentina.

I focused on getting and reporting the facts fully to the U.S. government. Proudly showing the support of my nation to the thousands of Argentines threatened by an outwardly sophisticated military junta gone "out of control" was my special responsibility — and my honor. Looking back on those terrible times, I know that one person can make a difference.

F. A. "Tex" Harris was Political Officer in Buenos Aires, Argentina, from 1977-79. Since joining the Foreign Service in 1965, he also served in Caracas, Venezuela; Washington, D.C., and Durban, South Africa. Since 1993, he has been President of AFSA.

'BLACKMAILING' PRESIDENT TOURE
GUINEA, 1975

By William Harrop

When I arrived as Chief of Mission to the Republic of Guinea in May, 1975, Sekou Toure, the father of "African Socialism," had been president for 17 years. He had created a repressive communist dictatorship. Guinea was a favorite of Moscow: The Soviets had built the university, the airfield, a railroad, a bauxite industry. The USSR had furnished advanced military equipment, technicians and training. The Soviet Embassy in Conakry had a staff of 950, the American Embassy just 15. Volunteers from the U.S. Peace Corps had just been expelled.

Huge TU-95 bombers (called "Bears" by NATO intelligence), configured for electronic surveillance, began to regularly refuel in Conakry, Guinea's capital. Operating among Moscow, Conakry and the other Soviet clients of Angola and Cuba, the bombers tracked — and occasionally harassed — the NATO fleet in the North Atlantic. I protested to President Toure about Guinea's participation in the Cold War by authorizing these flights, but to no avail. An admirer of John F. Kennedy, he insisted Guinea was non-aligned despite his ideological affinity for the Soviet bloc. But he was too beholden to the Russians to deny them military landing rights.

I looked for a source of leverage to force his hand without causing a break in relations. The answer was obvious. Because of the collapse of food production under Sekou Toure's strictly enforced collective farming, Guinea had become dependent upon American food aid under Public Law 480. American commodities were "sold" to the Guinean government for non-convertible local currency. The United States possessed huge accounts of essentially worthless Guinean sylis, as we did of Polish zlotys and Indian rupees.

Knowing that it would be difficult for the Carter administration to authorize an explicit link between humanitarian assistance and U.S. security concerns, I acted on my own to string out the annual PL-480 negotiations, all the while reminding Toure that permitting the TU-95 Bear flights was a hostile act against the Western Alliance and the United States. Toure, who liked to communicate with his people through public billboards, mounted signs which cried "Down with Food Blackmail." But he stopped the Bear flights, and our fleet was relieved of Soviet surveillance.

William Harrop was Ambassador to Guinea, from 1975-77. He joined the Foreign Service in 1954. Before he retired in 1993, his 39-year career included assignments in Palermo, Italy; Rome, Italy; Brussels, Belgium; Lubumbashi, Zaire; Canberra, Australia; Nairobi, Kenya; Tel Aviv, Israel; and in Washington, D.C., as an Inspector in the Inspector General's Office.

ARABIAN GULF BORDER CROSSING
SAUDI ARABIA, 1990

By Les Hickman

Years of living overseas had conditioned my body not to overreact to a ringing telephone in the middle of the night. My friends and relatives never could figure out the various time zones, and so the piercing of night quiet by the ringing phone had become surprisingly routine. The early morning of Aug. 2, 1990, however, was different. When the phone rang at 5 a.m., about an hour into rapid eye movement, I sat bolt upright, heart thumping, and fumbled for the instrument. "Les, I need you to come to the office as soon as possible," said the gravelly voice, which I recognized as that of Consul General Ken Stammerman. When I arrived at the consulate, I realized with a jarring surge of adrenaline, that the Emergency Action Committee was gathering. We were in the midst of a crisis.

Until that moment, my duty in Saudi Arabia had proceeded at a comfortable pace, allowing me time devoted to reflection and strategic thought without rushing to meet constant deadlines. No more. The second Stammerman uttered the words, "Iraq invaded Kuwait last night," I recognized the need for immediate action: quick, decisive, pure and simple. My assignment: Go to the Saudi-Kuwait border, evaluate the situation and assist U.S. government and private Americans fleeing Kuwait.

With an edgy rush produced by the mixture of fear and excitement, I threw some water bottles in a cooler and, with Deputy Principal Officer Jim Ball, sped north. At the border, we saw furious movement of people and vehicles entering Saudi Arabia, but even those with family in Kuwait were not allowed to enter the besieged country. Fortunately, we were acquainted with the Amir, Khalid Al-Otaishan. Earlier in the year, several colleagues and I had accepted his invitation for a weekend of desert camping, and now he was surprised to see us and concerned for our safety. He promptly assigned us a guard and assisted us in setting up an office at the Khafji Beach Hotel, the only available lodgings. There, we created a control room, established direct communication with the U.S. Consulate in Dhahran and decided to do five-hour shifts from the hotel to the border area. I took the first shift at the hotel and Ball exited out the back to avoid the guard, who had quickly lost interest in us.

As we monitored the border, we saw throngs of people setting up makeshift camps, waiting to enter Saudi Arabia. Only Saudis and Kuwaitis were permitted to cross the border without travel documents. Citizens of other countries without visas could do nothing but camp at the border and listen to the rumbling of Iraqi gunfire.

As the only foreign consular officials in Al-Khafji, we tried to help citizens of other Western nations, including Britons, Germans and Canadians, until consuls of other missions arrived from Riyadh two days later. So for five days, wearing the same clothes that we would rinse and dry in the hotel bathroom, we managed to help 250 Americans — and an unknown number of other Westerners — out of Kuwait. It was only after the flow of people slowed to a trickle that I looked up, through binoculars, and saw Iraqi soldiers digging up the road on the Kuwait border. Now, nothing separated us from the Iraqi army but air and opportunity. What I learned later was even more alarming: Units of the U.S. 82nd Airborne had formed a defensive line 60 miles south of Al-Khafji. We stood sandwiched between two powerful, opposing forces. After a week with no movement on either side, I returned to Al-Khafji alone.

Another exodus from Kuwait ensued. Now, however, only the elderly, women and children were allowed to leave, mostly Kuwaitis. This wave lasted about a week. I remained for another week in case U.S. embassy personnel in Kuwait might escape and head to the Saudi border. Had they left the embassy building, they would have been taken directly to Baghdad. These officers, as well as other Americans, would remain inside the U.S. Embassy for 137 days, living on canned tuna and brackish water, before returning to the United States via Baghdad.

I returned to Dhahran as American forces were building up, and tensions in the region grew. And as the stalemate continued, eventually leading up to the "line in the sand" ultimatum to Saddam Hussein, the unknown became more and more ominous. The dark clouds of the Desert Storm war were approaching.

Les Hickman was Chief of the Consular Section in Dhahran, Saudi Arabia, from 1989-92. Since joining the Foreign Service in 1978, he has served also in Caracas, Venezuela; Manila, the Philippines; Washington, D.C.; Bombay, India; and in the Sinai Desert in Egypt.

WITNESS TO WAR
CROATIA, 1995

By Susan Crais Hovanec

The war in the Balkans, which in 1991-95 unfolded before the world from the front pages of newspapers and the flickering screens of televisions, demonstrated one important point: Traditional diplomacy, even when supported by military force, doesn't always do the job. Sometimes it's simply not enough to formally petition governments to respect human rights, and sometimes getting the message to the public is the key to saving lives. This was one of those times.

Immediately following the Croatian government offensive in Western Slavonia on May 1, 1995, we had reports that thousands of civilians and combatants — Serbian and Croatian — had been killed, were fleeing or were advancing. Few reports were reliable; others suggested elderly people had been rounded up and placed in detention. Meanwhile we were certain thousands of innocent civilians were becoming refugees, with no place to go, no food to eat and no future to look forward to. We at the embassy knew our only hope to end the killing and ethnic cleansing in the region was to quickly determine the truth — and make sure the world heard it.

On May 8, 1995, the earliest date we at USIS received permission to enter the war-torn region, U.S. Ambassador Peter W. Galbraith and I set out, accompanied by more than 35 invited Western and local journalists, including representatives of CNN, ABC and CBS, The New York Times and The Los Angeles Times. Previously denied access, the media would be eyewitnesses for the world. Although active fighting had subsided, the situation was still volatile; we were fearful of snipers' bullets or detonating land mines.

Our goals were to reassure the civilians who remained in the area that the United States was ready to help, and to put the warring parties on notice that their conduct was being monitored and they would be held accountable. Before the news cameras, we placed flowers at the Holocaust monument at Jasenovac, demonstrating to a worldwide audience that the memorial still existed; we visited the detention centers and talked to refugees; we met with Croatian police and local Serb leaders and officials. We also visited a human rights center in Pakrac, set up by Croatian volunteer organizations with U.S. financial assistance to promote ethnic reconciliation during the conflict.

We achieved all our objectives: The media brought truth through its images and credible reports, and both warring parties got the "message" that the war should end. A bi-communal committee for local governance was formed on the spot. This was just one example of the benefits of direct communication and the media's role in today's high-tech age of instant communication — for example, the French wire service AFP and others filed their stories from our car telephone as we raced from site to site.

In my experience, the first victims in war are the very old, the very young and women. Another early casualty, as I witnessed in the Balkans, can be the truth. However, with a little help from U.S. Embassy personnel, we made sure that didn't happen this time.

Susan Crais Hovanec was Public Affairs Officer for USIA in Zagreb, Croatia, from 1992-95. Since joining the Foreign Service in 1976, she has served in Kinshasa, Zaire; Belgrade, Yugoslavia; and Mexico City, Mexico.

HOW TO SAVE A NATO BASE
ICELAND, 1974

By Frederick Irving

In late 1972 when I first came to the country as Ambassador, I began negotiations for retaining the U.S.-staffed NATO Anti-Submarine Naval Air Base in Iceland, but it would take a full two years and all the diplomatic skills I had acquired thus far in my career to achieve the goal.

The base, home to 3,400 U.S. military personnel and a handful of Canadians, had been located in Keflavik, about 40 miles east of the capital, Reykjavik, since 1951. Although no timetable had been set when the base was built, the early 1970s was a period of strong anti-NATO emotions in Iceland, and the issue became a major challenge in my career there. The climate was further complicated by the 1973-74 "Cod Wars" between England and Iceland after the latter declared a 50-mile fishing zone around the country, which was fiercely protested by the British as much wider than the 12-mile international standard. And in 1972, Iceland had just ushered in a new three-party coalition government, which included a Communist-oriented party. The coalition's platform called for shutting down the NATO base.

The base's significance is that Iceland's location in the North Atlantic is in such a strategic spot that submarine surveillance there permitted the United States to track Soviet nuclear submarines entering the Atlantic Ocean from the Kola Peninsula in the north. If the NATO base were lost, U.S. surveillance accuracy would be greatly diminished and the cost to establish and maintain an alternate site would be considerable. It should be noted that Iceland, while a NATO member, does not have a military of its own, does not want one, does not charge the United States rent for the base, and because of its proud and independent culture, has always maintained that, despite the obvious economic advantage, if Icelanders believed the base was no longer necessary, it wouldn't be allowed to remain.

The challenge to the U.S. Embassy staff was to influence the ministers and members of the Parliament to maintain the base, without being accused by Icelander officials of interfering in their country's internal affairs. The task was to openly persuade the three coalition parties and the general public that retaining the base was in their interests as well as that of the United States and NATO. In the almost two years of negotiations, the mutual respect and trust established between myself and the Icelandic government became very important.

Our embassy staff was small; including USIA, we numbered 11 Americans and 13 Icelanders; the Soviets had 77 Soviet nationals in their embassy in Reykjavik.

For two years, negotiations continued, sometimes on, sometimes off. Two of the Cabinet's seven ministers were pro-base, three were anti-base, one was leaning anti-base, the seventh was on the fence — leaving the Parliament about evenly divided.

U.S. Embassy spouses, on a voluntary and unpaid basis, of course, pitched in to accomplish our objectives. My wife, Dorothy, for example, calling on her professional skills as a teacher and community activist, developed many contacts with government, education and labor leaders, and other public opinion molders.

After two years, an agreement acceptable to the United States and Iceland was hammered out. Days before the formal agreement was to be signed, the Icelandic government did two unusual things. Because I had negotiated the agreement, Foreign Minister Einar Agustsson insisted I sign on behalf of the United States, rather than having a high official fly in from Washington, as is the usual practice. In addition, the Icelandic government publicly commended my wife as well as me for the role we played in the agreement's successful outcome, citing our "integrity and good will."

For me, this proved to be not only a professional challenge which was resolved to the advantage of U.S. security interests, but it was also a personal triumph, for my wife and I felt as warm toward the Icelanders as they did toward us.

Frederick Irving, who retired from the Foreign Service in 1979, was U.S. Ambassador to Iceland from 1972-76. In his 28-year career, he also served in Wellington, New Zealand; in Washington, D.C.; as DCM in Vienna, Austria; as Ambassador in Kingston, Jamaica; and as Assistant Secretary of State for the Bureau of Oceans and International Environmental and Scientific Affairs in Washington, D.C.

Too Many People
Indonesia, 1979-95

By Charles Johnson

I arrived in Jakarta, Indonesia, in 1979 to head USAID's Office of Population and to manage one of its largest and oldest population and family planning programs. In December 1995, I returned to Indonesia to head an evaluation of USAID's Private Sector Family Planning Project and observe the changes since 1975. Between 1968 and 1995, USAID spent about $300 million for population programs in Indonesia, helping to decrease the birthrate from 41 per 1,000 in 1970 to 25 per 1,000 in 1994, all of which reduced that island nation's rate of population growth by 39 percent within 27 years.

A decade earlier, in 1969, Indonesia seemed a poor bet for developing a successful national family planning program, since it didn't fit the pattern. In 1969, Indonesia was a poor country, with $50 annual per-capita income. Its 115 million people were mostly illiterate Moslem peasants living in rural areas spread over thousands of islands, who spoke hundreds of languages and had a myriad of differing cultures.

The Ministry of Health was politically weak, poorly staffed and had limited ability to reach the majority of people. The average couple had five or six children, so the population was growing more than 3 percent annually, doubling every 21 years. The island of Java supported two-thirds of the country's population in an area the size of Wisconsin. To match the population density of Java, all 5.5 billion inhabitants on Earth would have to be squeezed into the continental United States.

USAID began family planning assistance in Indonesia in 1968, offering limited support to a private organization working in a few of the country's largest cities. After the Indonesian National Family Planning Coordinating Board (BKKBN) was created in 1970, USAID assistance expanded. President Soeharto of Indonesia decreed that the first effort should be to bring family planning information and contraceptives to the rural areas of the country, home to more than 80 percent of the population. USAID helped BKKBN devise and test a plan to train village volunteers to provide information, condoms and oral contraceptives to their neighbors and to refer women to health centers for other contraceptive methods. Within a year, the pilot test proved so successful that BKKBN decided to extend the "village family planning" concept nationally. USAID provided funds to help BKKBN introduce village family planning on Java and Bali, later extending the program to all 27 provinces.

In its first nine years, the program was highly effective: Contraceptive use among married couples of reproductive age increased to 25 percent by 1979 — up from 5 percent in 1970.

In 1979, USAID developed a separate project with BKKBN to use family planning field workers and village volunteers to promote better maternal and child health and nutrition in villages that had already achieved at least 35 percent contraceptive prevalence. Family planning involved everyone in the village. Religious leaders were trained to weave family planning into their religious teachings. Within a year, it was clear that mothers in rural areas had begun to space their children or limit the number in their families; village volunteers, who by now had been convinced contraceptive use was accepted in the eyes of the Koran, were accepted by their neighbors as family planning providers.

Village leaders kept a map of each household identifying the contraceptive method being used. Family planning clubs were organized in each village for the "acceptors;" monthly meetings were organized to deal with complaints, to hold a small lottery to which each woman contributed, and to hear lectures on family planning, health, nutrition and job opportunities. Most groups' acceptors wore their village's individual colorful batik sarongs. Being an acceptor became a matter of pride.

To promote greater Indonesian self-sufficiency, we helped a government pharmaceutical company set up a contraceptive pill factory by buying specialized equipment and bringing in technical specialists to train Indonesians in the factory and to maintain high-quality control standards. The aim was to develop Indonesia contraceptive production so USAID could stop its huge annual contraceptive expense. With encouragement from USAID, factories began producing condoms and intra-uterine devices.

Lack of trained people hampered efforts to manage the rapidly expanding family planning program to all 27 provinces. So USAID set up a special program to send several hundred Indonesians to the United States for master's and doctoral degrees in public health, public administration, demographics and related fields. To strengthen Indonesian institutions, USAID-funded training for professors at four new schools of public health, as well as for the existing school.

When I visited Indonesia in 1995, much had changed from when I was last there in 1983. Major avenues in Jakarta now are lined with handsome 30- and 40-story office buildings; the streets are clogged with traffic; shopping centers rivaling the best in the United States cater to the rapidly growing middle and upper classes. Annual per-capita income now approaches $1,000. Private hospitals offer high-quality health care and health insurance is just around the corner.

The family planning program has changed as well. By 1994, the average woman was having 2.9 children; nearly 55 percent of all married couples of reproductive age were using contraceptives; and more than 28 percent of those couples now purchased their contraceptives rather than receiving them from the government, up from 12 percent in 1987. USAID promoted this shift to the private sector with a large project involving use of mass media advertising; trained private doctors, midwives and pharmacists in family planning; it urged professional associations of medical and health personnel to "think private sector."

For me, there's no question that in the nearly 28 years that USAID has been promoting family planning programs in Indonesia, the mission here has made a big difference.

Charles Johnson was Chief of the Office of Population at USAID in Jakarta, Indonesia, from 1979-83. Before retiring from the Foreign Service in 1989, he was posted in Santiago, Chile, and Washington, D.C.

HELPING FREE KIDNAPPED STUDENTS
TANZANIA, 1975

By Ron Johnston

One of the most interesting projects I worked on was in 1975, helping to free four student interns who had been kidnapped from primatologist Jane Goodall's research station on the remote Gombe Stream Reserve on the Tanzanian shores of Lake Tanganyika.

When 40 armed raiders came to her camp on May 20 and asked the African guard, "Where are the white people?" it became the start of an intense four-week period that required extended travel, logistics planning, substantial shipping and high-level negotiations with Washington. Little did I know what I was getting into.

As a communications and radio technician at U.S. Embassy Nairobi, I had been given vague and ambiguous instructions, directed only "to charter an aircraft south to Kigoma, Tanzania," and "to provide whatever assistance was necessary in establishing a radio communications network" in that area. I had been given very few details: Only later did I realize that I was becoming involved in a cross-border terrorist incident that would have international diplomatic ramifications.

When the twin engine aircraft landed on the dirt strip outside Kigoma, I was met by Tanzanian Park Service Director Derek Bryelson, who was also Goodall's husband, who drove me to the home of a U.S. shrimp research specialist. I also met another American diplomat from Zanzibar, who had been told to help me establish a radio base from which to conduct negotiations between Washington and local authorities. Together, we set up and manned the communications center, as police and other diplomats tried to determine the welfare and whereabouts of the kidnapped students — three Americans and a Dutchman. We set up a network to communicate with U.S. Ambassador Beverly Carter in Dar es Salaam, my office in Nairobi and neighboring U.S. embassies in East Africa.

After surveying the area and making a list of essentials, including food, I returned to Nairobi to assemble a communications package. Unlike today's portable satellite systems and cellular telephones, my equipment was large, heavy and not easy to use. It required several trips to bring it all in, and due to the remoteness of this village, I needed a great deal of Yankee ingenuity to install and activate the radios. We had commandeered the shrimp specialist's home as our base, and although he and his wife were exceptionally good hosts, they must have thought it strange that we chose to bunk in their home. It wasn't overly large but it did have electricity as well as windows. Within three to five days, the center was operating at full speed.

The kidnapped students had come to East Africa as summer interns to help Goodall in her chimpanzee research; she and 11 other interns had managed to escape unharmed and to alert authorities. At one point, at the air landing strip, I met an unkempt Goodall, who said something like, "Thank God you're here. Please get my interns back." Six days after the kidnapping, Ann Arbor, Mich., intern Barbara Smuts was released with instructions from the kidnappers, but only after several thousands of dollars had been paid in ransom. Initially, the kidnappers had demanded many hundreds of thousands of dollars, millions of rounds of ammunition, several amphibious boats and the release of dozens of Kenyan political prisoners.

At this point, intense negotiations were being conducted between Washington officials and local and U.S. officials in Zaire, Burundi and Kenya. On July 25, the remaining three students were released unharmed, after having spent four weeks in the Zairian jungle on the western side of Lake Tangyanika, while our camp was based on its eastern side. We never learned exactly what the kidnappers received in return for the students.

Today, Kigoma is still a small village on the shore of the lake and chimpanzee research still continues at Gombe, but the memories of those days in the East African bush remain quite vivid to me, and I was glad to have been part of a process that had a positive ending.

Ron Johnston was Communications-Electronics Officer in Nairobi, Kenya, from 1972-76. Since joining the Foreign Service in 1967, he has also served in Washington, D.C.; Accra, Ghana; and Bonn, Germany.

SILENCE OF THE LAMBS
AFGHANISTAN, 1966

By John Kean

In 1966 I was asked by Bill Macomber, USAID's Assistant Administrator for the Near East and South Asia, to get ready: I was going to Afghanistan. Becoming acquainted with Afghanistan, the largest USAID mission in the world at that time after Vietnam, was a gargantuan task. The office had 200-plus advisers, technicians and staff, including both contractors and direct-hire USAID employees. The United States was engaged in a wide range of activities, from emergency wheat shipments to head off potential famine during droughts to building roads and schools. We also were helping run a number of irrigation and agricultural projects and supported the development of the country's lone university.

We were working head-to-head against the Russians there as well, often competing in precisely the same field, sometimes duplicating one another's work, all with the full knowledge of the Afghan government. Afghan officials weren't stupid: They were perfectly willing to accept aid funds from both sides, knowing full well that their country was very much on the forefront of the Cold War struggle. No matter if it was transportation, education or telecommunications links, our government mission was intent on minimizing the country's dependency on the Soviet Union.

One of the things we did was to support the development of the *karakul* (Persian lamb) industry and to open up larger western markets for *karakul*. Export of this beautiful black curly fur was an excellent source of export earnings for Afghanistan. However, since World War II all *karakul* exports had been passing through the Soviet Union, being identified as Soviet products on the international fur market. So USAID tried to build a more efficient system and a more economical one of producing, cleaning, sorting and grading *karakul* pelts, setting up direct links to London and New York markets. Within two years, the government began earning between $15 million and $20 million annually on the sale of this product.

I remember a trip to Mazar-i-Sharif with a New York-based private *karakul* trader and processor. He was certain he would not survive this rough trip into the boondocks. At that time, Russians were still working on the main road, so we were driving over the rough, bumpy track, which took six hours to go only 100 miles. The U.S. *karakul* expert would not even eat an Afghan orange, fearful of becoming ill. However, his useful advice helped shift the *karakul* trade to Western channels within five years, a move that helped minimize Afghans' dependency on the Soviets for channeling and marketing *karakul*.

John Kean was USAID's Assistant Director for Development Planning in Kabul, Afghanistan, from 1966-68. Before retiring from the Foreign Service in 1978, Kean's 35-year career also included postings in Ankara, Turkey; Cairo, Egypt; Karachi, Pakistan; and Accra, Ghana.

TIE A YELLOW RIBBON
IRAN, 1979-81

By L. Bruce Laingen

For me, looking back on almost 40 years in the Foreign Service is to see a kaleidoscope of experiences that a farm boy from Minnesota could not conceivably have imagined. Issuing visas, at times around the clock, at a displaced persons camp in postwar Germany; flying the U.S. flag as consul in a listening post at Meshed, close to the then-Soviet border of Iran; escorting First Lady Jackie Kennedy on her 1962 triumphal tour of Pakistan; watching President Lyndon Johnson invite Anwar, the Pakistani camel driver, to visit the United States; observing the Indo/Pakistan War of 1971 that saw the birth of Bangladesh; and sailing in the magnificent Grand Harbor of the island republic of Malta.

But one assignment is etched forever in my mind: my second tour in Iran, in 1979-81, when I became a candidate for the Guiness Book of Records — the only chief of a diplomatic mission to lose his embassy and its entire staff to political terrorists supported by their government, and to be held hostage for political purposes for more than a year. This was arguably the most egregious violation of the traditions and principles of diplomatic immunity in the history of diplomacy.

In America's experience with the Iranian Revolution that began in 1979, there are volumes of remembrances — and lessons: The need in times of political uncertainty to challenge conventional wisdom; my staff's endurance with dignity; the heroism and sacrifice of those men who put their lives on the line to restore us hostages to freedom but whose flying machines failed them; and being reminded of our good fortune in a neighbor, Canada, which was ready to set aside all its interests in Iran to bring six Americans home to safety.

But perhaps we should remember the way this crisis also triggered what became a class act of the best of community across our country. Beginning with an understandable outburst of anger and hate, much of it unfortunately directed at Iranians living in America, there evolved a most remarkable spirit of national unity — an outpouring of caring symbolized by flags, prayers, church bells, an avalanche of mail, and above all that ubiquitous yellow ribbon, that became and remains today the universal symbol of caring for fellow American in distress.

For a time, at least, there was also a new appreciation by the American public of the role played by their diplomats abroad in areas of stress and danger. Since then others in the Foreign Service have continued that role, often on the front lines in defense of American interests — in Beirut, Kuwait, Somalia — and today, in new countries born of the former Soviet Union, of whose freedom my Foreign Service generation could only dream 40 years ago. Today I tell all who are new to the Foreign Service: Welcome to the ultimate in adventure, and in public service.

L. Bruce Laingen, who retired from the Foreign Service in 1987, was Chief of Mission in Tehran, Iran, from 1979-81. In his 38-year career, he also served in Hamburg, Germany; Washington, D.C.; Karachi, Pakistan; Kabul, Afganhistan; and as Ambassador to Valletta, Malta.

FIGHTING OFF PROTESTORS
HAITI, 1993

By Luis Moreno

By October 1993, the chaotic political situation in Haiti was about to reach the boiling point. The illegal de facto military government, which had overthrown the democratically elected government of President Jean Bertrand Aristide in September 1991, was wavering on promises made during the negotiations that past summer at Governor's Island. The crippling international embargo had brought the military junta to the table, and promises had been made for the eventual restoration of democracy to the island nation. One of the key provisions of the agreement was the docking of the U.S. Naval Ship *Harlan County*, with 200 U.S. Special Forces advisers, scheduled for Oct. 15. Opponents of democracy were dead set against the landing. In early October, Chargé d'Affaires Vicki Huddleston assigned Coast Guard Attache Dave Breuninger and me to coordinate the ship's docking at the lone Port-au-Prince facility. When several U.N. security agents and I arrived at sunrise that Oct. 15 to prepare for the ship's 10 a.m. VIP ceremony, the port was eerily silent, despite rumors that military-backed Haitian gangsters would try to prevent the docking. However, a massive Cuban freighter was berthed in the space reserved for the *Harlan County*, though there was no sign of life on the vessel. As I prepared to board it, we were met by a dozen armed and extremely drunken Haitian toughs, who identified themselves as "attachés." Extremely nervous, the "attachés" insisted that we leave, promising that there would be no "U.S. invasion."

The three U.N. agents quickly left the dock, and I pretended to leave, though I ducked instead into a nearby office to radio the U.S. Embassy, which rapidly dispatched my partner, Dave Breuninger, who literally barreled his four-wheel drive vehicle through the port's wire-fence entrance, as the toughs vainly tried to lock the massive gates. After we linked up, we eluded the enraged four or five gate guards and headed for the office of National Port Director Max Paul, prepared to demand that the Cuban freighter leave the slip and the *Harlan County* be allowed to dock.

As we approached Paul's office, we were confronted by several shotgun-wielding port guards. We pushed the shotguns aside, and, praying they had no ammunition, we mounted the stairway and tried to enter Paul's office. Unfortunately, the door was barred by a group of angry female employees, many of whom threw themselves against the door, shouting that they preferred death to an "American occupation" and the return of Aristide. We returned to the port area and watched as the Port Captain organized hundreds of waiting Haitian men to pose as anti-American demonstrators, posting them in strategic positions around the port area.

Breuninger and I continued to radio reports to the embassy, and finally recommended that the VIP ceremony be canceled, with the docking of the vessel becoming more doubtful every second. At this point, Huddleston and another embassy Political Officer had decided to try to enter the port area, but her fully armored embassy car was held up for nearly 90 minutes, as protestors smashed it with bricks and rocks.

By this time, we were playing cat and mouse with the "attachés" on the dock. Since we thought that keeping the embassy informed of developments was more important that saving our hides, we continued to elude the Haitians, staying one step ahead of them along the docks. At one point, I hid briefly on the ship of the bewildered Cuban crew, who appeared to be reluctant players in the unfolding drama. At about noon, the *Harlan County* edged over the horizon, a sight that prompted a spontaneous demonstration of shouting, clapping — and alarmingly, gunfire — by protestors, who now numbered a couple of hundred. I'll never forget the sight of a mini-skirted secretary, in total euphoria, firing a pistol in every direction. We finally were able to escape.

Although the *Harlan County* would not be allowed to dock that day, it would only be a short-term victory for the Haitian military. Another year of the crippling international embargo, and thousands of migrants and hundreds of dead human rights victims later, 20,000 multinational troops would finally land in the Caribbean nation on Sept. 10, 1994, ensuring that democracy would be restored to Haiti. But we would not easily forget the events of Oct. 15, 1993.

Luis Moreno was Refugee Coordinator at U.S. Embassy Port-au-Prince, Haiti, from 1993-95. Since he joined the Foreign Service in 1983, his other posts have included Bogota, Colombia; Managua, Nicaragua; Lima, Peru; Washington, D.C., and Panama City, Panama.

THE SHAH AND THE CUBAN MISSILE CRISIS
TEHRAN, 1962

By Dan Newberry

In October 1962, when the Cuban Missile Crisis was gripping the world, I was the Deputy Political Counselor in U.S. Embassy Tehran. Like many colleagues in the embassy and in the diplomatic corps, I was engulfed in the dread that a third world war could break out at any moment. The Shah of Iran, too, felt that dread, Ambassador Julius Holmes told us after one of his daily audiences with His Imperial Majesty.

The monarch wanted to be kept informed, and we all knew he was very touchy about anything that smacked of his being taken for granted by the U.S. government. He had sent personal messages of solidarity to President John F. Kennedy but he was unable to forget that the Soviet Union was positioned 300 miles to the north of Tehran, across the border in the Azerbaijan, S.S.R., now the independent republic of Azerbaijan.

The Shah had been on his throne only a few years, when in 1946, the Red Army occupied Iranian Azerbaijan. President Harry Truman had sent the Russians packing in 1946 with an ultimatum that in retrospect marked the beginning of the Cold War. But then the USSR did not have the atom bomb.

Now in 1962, President Kennedy was struggling with quite a different equation. A misstep could make a reality out of the Shah's — and our — nightmare, but it was unlikely to bring bombs raining on Tehran. A more likely scenario would be a revolt inspired by Soviet sympathizers, with far more bloody consequences than those of a decade earlier in the Mossadegh era. Of course, the Shah wanted to be kept informed and not through a third party, such as Iran's Washington Embassy.

It happened that I was on one-week rotation as Duty Officer for U.S. Embassy Tehran when, the Cuban Missile Crisis came to a climax. Being Duty Officer meant that I was on call to come into the Chancery and deal with any urgent business after regular working hours, if I could not resolve the matter by telephone. Particularly bracing were the recurring occasions when "night action" telegrams were received by the embassy's Communications Center. A very tense Communicator called me at home at about midnight in late November 1962 to alert me that Washington had warned of a long presidential message due in shortly. He inquired if he should alert the sleeping Ambassador Julius Holmes at his home. I suggested he wait until I could see the message myself and determine if it was important enough to wake the Ambassador.

It took me a half hour to reach the Chancery and by the time I reached the Communications Center, the segmented message was coming in reverse order, so I had to wait an hour and a half for the message to be decrypted and I could read the instructions. It turned out to be a worldwide "circular" telegram, but we dressed it up to appear as a personal message from President Kennedy to the Shah. It was the bare outline of the president's forthcoming proclamation of a naval quarantine against Soviet shipping headed for Cuba — which basically meant the Caribbean was off-limits to Soviet ships — and U.S. assurances to Moscow that the United States would not invade Cuba. There was no reassurance that Washington expected a peaceable reply from Moscow. The White House announcement would be public in a matter of hours, just about when the Shah would be having his breakfast.

After waking the Ambassador about 2 a.m. and discussing the telegram with him, I was instructed to rouse someone at the palace to get permission to bring the message directly to the Shah. All to no avail: I finally drove to the palace myself and delivered it to the captain of the guard. Without revealing the message's contents, I underscored that it had to be delivered before the Shah had his Imperial Breakfast and before His Majesty turned on the radio. Replied the captain, "That depends on His Majesty."

Dan Newberry, who retired from the Foreign Service in 1985, was Deputy Political Counselor from 1962-64 in U.S. Embassy Tehran, Iran. In his 37-year career, he also served in Jerusalem, Israel; Istanbul, Turkey; Vientiane, Laos; Adana, Turkey; Tangier, Morocco; Dhaka, Bangladesh; and Ankara, Turkey.

A New Era For Human Rights
Botswana, 1977

By Donald Norland

My assignment as Ambassador to Botswana, Lesotho and Swaziland coincided with the election of Jimmy Carter as president — and an unprecedented emphasis on human rights in U.S. foreign relations — which began immediately after his inauguration in January 1977.

During frequent official and social meetings with Botswana President Sir Seretse Khama, I soon realized that he had acquired unquestioned democratic credentials, as a result of his Oxford education and life under British colonialism. This was confirmed by the political climate, which contrasted sharply with that of a number of other African countries I had come to know, most notably Guinea, with its Stalinist brutalities.

But it was 1977, and for most Americans and U.S. bureaucrats, Africa was still the dark continent. The idea of applying U.S. standards of democracy and human rights to African countries was generally regarded as not only wildly idealistic, but seriously misguided given the United States' central all-embracing mission of opposing and defeating communism. But since the Carter administration let it be known that a country's human rights record would be consulted in judging USAID funding requests, a new practical incentive emerged for focusing carefully on human rights conditions.

So we made human rights a priority item for all staff at U.S. Embassy Gaborone. I personally made a point of calling on the leaders of all opposition political parties and, in the course of each conversation, asked whether each leader had any hesitation in campaigning or in expressing their opposing views freely, either in Parliament, party meetings or media. The response was unanimous: No one felt inhibited, either by government officials or by police. I double checked with media representatives, leading business owners and leaders of local NGOs. The reply was the same — and we at the embassy began to say so repeatedly in reports to Washington

Within a year, after some initial skepticism, the idea that Botswana was both free and democratic in the full sense of the word began to gain acceptance. Botswana gradually became recognized as a model, indeed as proof, that African countries could be judged by the same standards as other democracies. When Assistant Secretary for Human Rights and Humanitarian Affairs Pat Derian prepared her first travel to Africa in 1977, her main speech was to be in Gaborone. Regrettably illness forced Derian to cancel the trip, but Botswana's record and that of President Khama began to speak for themselves — and do to this day. While difficult to measure, a part of Botswana's record of political stability and economic success in the nearly 30 years since independence in 1966 is now generally attributed to U.S. leadership in recognizing — and providing timely encouragement to — its democratic government and exemplary human rights record.

Donald Norland was Ambassador to Botswana, Lesotho and Swaziland from 1976-79. Before he retired from the Foreign Service in 1981, his 29-year career also included postings in Rabat, Morocco; Abidjan, Côte d'Ivoire; Paris, France; The Hague, The Netherlands; Conakry, Guinea; and N'Djamena, Chad.

PAVING THE WAY FOR WOMEN
WASHINGTON, D.C., 1995

By Phyllis E. Oakley

I am constantly amazed at the changes in women's demeanor as I walk though the State Department. Today's female FSOs look sharp, determined and confident, a far cry from what I remember of myself and a few intrepid friends from graduate school when we dared to brave the male bastion that was the 1957 State Department. Indeed, I was the only woman in my orientation class of 30.

I recall how I felt at that time, not quite sure how I would be treated and as something of an interloper, a brazen intruder, if you will, trying to put a female presence in the Foreign Service, a career so clearly dominated and controlled by men.

Also, I did exactly what had been foretold would happen if the Foreign Service started to accept more women: I met and became engaged to another FSO. My consciousness being at the prevailing low level of the time, it didn't occur to me to protest or fight the unspoken rule that required women officers who married to resign their posts. And so I resigned, prepared my trousseau, wed Bob Oakley in Cairo — thanks to a ticket from my father — and we started our great adventure to his postings in the Sudan, Ivory Coast, Vietnam, Paris, New York and Beirut. By 1962, we had two children in tow.

By then, it was the early '60s, and America was changing. There was a sexual revolution, a feminist revolution, a political revolution — thanks to Vietnam — and even the State Department changed. To avoid discrimination lawsuits, in 1974, the State Department offered re-entry to women like me, female FSOs who chose to come back to the Foreign Service.

I found it a great advantage to be a woman in the mid-'70s. Officials were striving to advance women and to demonstrate that they were moving with the times. I became the first female staff assistant on the Seventh Floor, the first spouse permitted to work in her husband's embassy in Kinshasa and the first woman spokeswoman in the State Department. It has been a rewarding path — providing both time for my children when they were young and a fulfilling career.

I understand that entering classes of the Foreign Service now have a majority of women. I now see women in meetings presenting their views without a hint of deferral to men or a desire to hold back. I attend sessions where women dominate and sometimes make up the entire staff. And tandem couples — in which both spouses are FSOs — have become commonplace.

There is no way I can describe how different all this is from when I began as the only woman in my A-100 class in September 1957. If change is the mark of life, there may be hope yet for the Foreign Service.

Phyllis E. Oakley became one of the first women appointed to high-level management in the State Department. She served as State's Deputy Spokesman from 1986-89, as Deputy Assistant Secretary for Regional Analysis in the Bureau of Intelligence and Research from 1991-93, and as Assistant Secretary of the Bureau of Population, Refugees and Migration since 1994. Since rejoining the Foreign Service in 1974, her foreign posts have included Kinshasa, Zaire, and Islamabad, Pakistan.

AVERTING FAMINE FOR 18 MILLION
SOUTHERN AFRICA, 1993

By Lois Richards

In early 1992, frightening weather warnings, including low rainfall collection, weather imaging satellite reports, warmer than usual temperatures and on-the-ground USAID mission reporting indicated that the century's worst drought was devastating southern Africa's maize crop. The drought threatened production of this corn-based staple crop in the region's 10 countries — Angola, Botswana, Malawi, Mozambique, Namibia, South Africa, Swaziland, Lesotho, Zambia and Zimbabwe — by between 40 to 60 percent in most countries and up to 90 percent in others. Only South Africa could afford to replace its lost production with imports.

Also, despite a well developed road and rail system on the southern section of the continent, fears grew of a massive logistics logjam and delayed food deliveries, due to the massive amounts of imports required for a region with six landlocked nations. If sufficient food did not arrive by September, when stocks would be depleted, 18 million people faced serious famine.

A famine would complicate life in other ways by producing massive refugee problems and threatening to disrupt major U.S.-supported political and economic reforms under way in many affected states. Namibia was newly independent; South Africa was in transition to a black majority government; Zambia and Zimbabwe were undertaking recommended reforms.

Alerted by the unprecedented early warnings — systems had never before been this sophisticated — USAID's Bureau for Humanitarian Response (BHR) collaborated with the Africa Bureau (AFR) and the State Department to mount a massive U.S. response. By May and June, food — two-thirds alone from U.S. Department of Agriculture surpluses in storehouses in the States — started flowing into the region, thanks to a U.S.-led coalition of donors worldwide.

By late 1992, signs were evident the famine had been averted — the first time such a severe drought had not led directly to widespread famine. And while the relief effort was costly, it would have been more expensive had the famine erupted. My involvement in this successful U.S.-led international relief effort was one of the most satisfying events in my 30-year government career.

Lois Richards was Deputy Assistant Administrator in the Office of the Assistant Administrator in the Bureau for Humanitarian Response at USAID from 1992-95. Before retiring from the Service in 1995, her 30-year career included postings in Mogadishu, Somalia; Monrovia, Liberia; Amman, Jordan; Nairobi, Kenya; Accra, Ghana; and Lagos, Nigeria.

THE UNAPPRECIATED CONSULAR OFFICER
WASHINGTON, D.C., 1995

By Mary A. Ryan

Consular Officers are the unsung heroes of the Department of State. Singularly unappreciated by an organization that prizes political reporting above all other skills, Consular Officers around the world, day in and day out, make a difference in the lives of Americans abroad. They win the Department of State numerous friends and, in fact, have developed its only real constituency: the traveling American public.

Often considered by career diplomats as the specialty that leads nowhere, consular work remains the most noble of all Foreign Service tasks because it concerns the individual, the person who needs help, be it the American who needs aid in getting his wife's body to Missouri after she died of a heart attack in Cameroon, or the Israeli in Tel Aviv seeking an immigrant visa to live in the United States. The Consular Section officers are the first, and sometimes the only, people who represent America to foreigners abroad. They are at the front line.

Every day, American citizens send my office thank-you notes for the work of Consular Officers. One woman wrote in mid-1995 of her gratitude to the Consular Officer who helped unsnag a serious problem that had halted the adoption process of a baby girl in China. The Consul not only untangled and finally broke the red tape, he took first her and later the baby into his house when the process crept into its second month and her money began to run out. Today, that baby is a happy toddler just learning to walk.

A wife wrote of the terror of hearing that her husband had suffered a heart attack in Turkmenistan, a country halfway around the world, and of her relief when the U.S. Embassy's Consular Officer called to say she had visited him in the hospital, finally joining the spouse via telephone call.

Consular Officers, both Foreign Service and Civil Service, worked around the clock during the 1990 crisis in Kuwait, when the country was invaded by Iraq. They contacted the American families of the dozens of "human shields," relaying information between Kuwait and the Consular Sections of U.S. embassies in other Middle East posts. They worked tirelessly, helping to evacuate American citizens, being available day and night to comfort distraught relatives, and finally, witnessing those planeloads of rescued flying into Washington, D.C., to be reunited with loved ones.

When Hurricane Luis ravaged the Caribbean in October 1995, two Consular Officers of the Bureau of Consular Affairs's "fly-away teams" walked the damaged island of St. Maarten, sleeping on the ground and missing meals for 10 days until every one of the several thousand visiting American citizens was accounted for. These "fly-away teams," groups of between two and 10 people on constant call, commit themselves to going anywhere in the world at a moment's notice, whenever an overseas disaster threatens Americans.

Thirty years ago, public service was considered a noble profession. Today, after years of politicians' denigration of Washington's "bureaucrats," the psychic rewards of a public service career are few. Yet the Department of State and the Foreign Service are still able to attract committed, dedicated, hardworking men and women who continue to believe that the United States is the greatest country on earth and that there is no worthier work than to serve the U.S. government and the American people. The author O. Henry put it best: "You can't appreciate home 'til you've left it, nor Old Glory 'til you see it hanging on a broomstick on a shanty of a Consul in a foreign town."

Mary A. Ryan has been Assistant Secretary of State for Consular Affairs in Washington, D.C., since 1993. Since joining the Foreign Service in 1966, she also has served in Naples, Italy; Tegucigalpa, Honduras; Monterrey, Mexico; Abidjan, Côte d'Ivoire; Khartoum, Sudan; and as Ambassador in Mbabane, Swaziland.

EARTHQUAKE!
COSTA RICA, 1991

By Ronald F. Venezia

The rumble always precedes the shake. We at USAID were on the third floor of a concrete building in San Jose, Costa Rica, when the upheaval that raised the Caribbean coast by six feet in 40 seconds announced itself as a distant roar. The rocking jolts about 4:10 p.m. that day in April 1991 sent me reaching for my gyrating computer while bookshelves unburdened themselves and screaming colleagues dove under their desks. In a country of constant tremors, this was The Big One. What then unfolded was a textbook case of disaster response by an embassy team armed with excellent leadership and an up-to-date disaster relief plan.

For starters, we could depend on the Regional USAID Office of Foreign Disaster Assistance, which happened to be based in San Jose, led by Regional Director Paul Bell. He and his team had led many training sessions for the Costa Rican government's Emergency Response Committee, and it now looked like the preparation would pay off. At an emergency meeting immediately after the quake, attended by Bell and Richard Burke, USAID Costa Rica's experienced Disaster Relief Officer, it was determined that most of San Jose had survived the tremor, which measured 6.8 on the Richter scale. But the news was not so good for the eastern shore.

The earthquake's epicenter was off the country's eastern coast, with the worst damage in the tiny strategic port town of Limon, where dozens had been killed, 20,000 had been displaced and key port buildings had been destroyed. Because the capital's lone airport had no lights, evening flights were impossible, but a USAID team was on a chartered airplane to Limon the next morning to investigate the damage and to determine if any Americans had been affected. Just behind us was President Rafael Calderon and his entourage, whose plane, like ours, had to narrowly skirt the airstrip's wide cracks.

Once on the ground, President Calderon invited me to accompany his group in his car to inspect the area. We saw how widespread the damage was: a kaput oil refinery; several downed bridges that had once linked the port to dozens of coastal towns and economic zones; a hospital that had to be condemned; miles of roadway with deep, jagged gouges; the country's most important port destroyed; and countless damaged buildings and homes. However, we soon determined that the most serious toll was economic, not human.

Thousands of people dependent on Costa Rica's major export of bananas faced immediate unemployment. The Costa Ricans needed help — and they needed it quickly. Within 36 hours of the quake, a team of six Panama-based engineers from the U.S. Army Corps of Engineers was on the ground, working with Burke and two USAID engineers round the clock to determine which key bridges and roads needed immediate repair. Within three days, preliminary engineering drawings were ready, and we surveyed the suggested repairs, and considered its price tag of several million dollars.

USAID San Jose recommended that the United States provide $5 million for the relief effort, with the local USAID mission using $2 million in program funds. Another $3 million could be provided from the OFDA's $25 million worldwide annual emergency fund in Washington. Within another two days the grant money was available, and a scant two weeks after the quake had hit, a contract was signed with the Army Corps of Engineers for the repairs to begin. Permanent repairs were completed within six months.

We on the Country Team took immense pride in how well the system worked: With good will, experienced leadership, staff support, good planning and a little luck, we produced something that showed the U.S. government and America at its best.

Ronald F. Venezia was USAID Mission Director from 1990-94 in San Jose, Costa Rica. Before retiring in 1994, his 30-year career also included postings in Guatemala City, Guatemala; Santa Domingo, Dominican Republic, and Tegucigalpa, Honduras.

MY COTTON PICKIN' JOB
EGYPT, 1976-78

By Reiter Webb

My first job on arriving in Cairo in 1976 was to convince Ambassador Hermann Eilts that an Agricultural Attaché could be of help to the embassy, which had only been a U.S. Interests Section since President Gamal Abdel Nasser broke off diplomatic relations with the United States following the 1967 war. Those were exciting days in Egypt. We started from scratch in an office with only a brass plaque, one phone and 35 U.S. FSOs, U.S. Marine guards and communicators. I was to report on production, consumption and trade in Egypt's agricultural sector. I was not yet an FSO because during the late 1970s, FAS was not considered part of the Foreign Service, although in 1981 we all automatically became FSOs.

For the first six months I was at post, we worked seven days a week, 12 hours a day; no one at the embassy took off a single day. It was a very tiresome, very difficult assignment. Later, as more people joined the embassy staff, we were still 35 people doing the work of 250, with the entire staff sharing three cars for two years. Our living conditions were poor: One of us was sick from food poisoning every month; the traffic situation was horrendous, with too many cars producing too much pollution. However, Egyptians were warm, friendly and pro-American.

Market development was our post's central theme and the key crop here was cotton. Egyptian cotton was worth twice the price of U.S. cotton because it was "long-stapled," which means it could be exported to Paris at high prices for fine dresses. However, Egyptians choose instead to keep it at home, using it to produce cotton socks and towels. At that time, Egypt was exporting only about half its 20 million bales of cotton a year, at $2 a pound, to the United States and Western Europe.

Our office advised the Egyptians to import medium- and short- stapled cottons at $1 a pound from the United States to produce its everyday clothing and to export their own high-quality cotton at double the price. Initially, we had limited success with this strategy, because Egyptian producers feared they would import foreign pests along with the foreign cotton. And although I took Egyptian authorities to Long Beach, Calif., several times to demonstrate high-quality U.S. fumigation facilities for cotton and to convince them that imported cotton proved no risk, it would take several long months before they finally agreed to attempt cotton imports. However, this policy change was a huge success for Egyptians, helping to double the country's foreign trade earnings and earning Egypt a worldwide reputation as a maker of high-quality cotton. ■

Reiter Webb was Agricultural Attaché in Cairo, Egypt, from 1976-78. In his 30-plus-year career, he also served in London, England.

ABBREVIATIONS,

ABBREVIATIONS AND ACRONYMS

(APEC) Asia Pacific Economic Cooperation
(ASEAN) Association of Southeast Asian Nations
(CIA) Central Intelligence Agency
(CINCCENT) Commander in Chief, Central Command
(CINCEUR) Commander in Chief, European Command
(CINCPAC) Commander in Chief, Pacific Command
(CINCSOUTH) Commander in Chief, Southern Command
(CODEL) Congressional Delegation (from Washington)
(CU) Bureau of Educational and Cultural Affairs (formerly in State, now in USIA)
(DEA) U.S. Drug Enforcement Agency
(DFA) Department of Foreign Affairs (of a foreign country)
(DAO) Defense Attache Office
(DOD) U.S. Department of Defense
(EPA) U.S. Environmental Protection Agency
(FAA) Federal Aviation Administration
(FAAS) Foreign Affairs Administrative Support System
(FAS) Foreign Agricultural Service
(FBI) Federal Bureau of Investigation
(FBIS) Foreign Broadcast Information Service
(FODAG) U.S. Mission to the United Nations Agencies for Food and Agriculture
(FS) Foreign Service
(GAO) Government Accounting Office
(GLOBE) Global Learning and Observation to Benefit the Environment
(GNP) Gross National Product
(HHS) Health and Human Services
(ICA) U.S. International Communications Agency (former name of USIA)
(ICAO) U.S. Mission to the International Civil Aviation Organization
(ICITAP) International Criminal Investigative Training and Assistance Program
(IMET) International Military Education and Training
(INS) Immigration and Naturalization Service
(IPTF) International Police Task Force
(IRS) Internal Revenue Service
(JCS) Joint Chiefs of Staff

(MAP) Military Assistance Program
(NASA) National Aeronautical and Space Administration
(NFATC) National Foreign Affairs Training Center
(NIS) New Independent States
(NIV) Non-Immigrant Visa
(NGOs) Non-Governmental Organizations
(NSC) National Security Council
(OECD) Organization for Economic Cooperation and Development
(OFDA) Office of Foreign Disaster Assistance
(OPIC) Overseas Private Investment Corp.
(PAHO) Pan American Health Organization
(RAMC) Regional Administrative Management Center
(SGSO) Supervisory General Services Office
(SSA) U.S. Social Security Administration
(UN) United Nations
(UNESCO) U.S. Observer Mission to the United Nations Educational Scientific and Cultural Organization
(UNHCR) United Nations High Commission on Refugees
(UN Geneva) U.S. Mission to the Geneva Office of the United Nations
(UNVIE) U.S. Mission to the Vienna Office of the United Nations
(USACOM) U.S. Atlantic Command
(USAF) U.S. Air Force
(USAID) U.S. Agency for International Development
(USDA) U.S. Department of Agriculture
(USEU) U.S. Mission to the European Union
(USIA) U.S. Information Agency
(USIS) U.S. Information Service (USIA overseas)
(USNATO) U.S. Mission to the North Atlantic Treaty Organization
(USOAS) U.S. Mission to the Organization of American States
(USOECD) U.S. Mission to the Organization for Economic Cooperation and Development
(USTR) U.S. Trade Representative's Office
(USUN) U.S. Mission to the United Nations
(USVIE) U.S. Mission to the Vienna Office of the United Nations
(VA) Veterans Administration
(/W) Washington Office of Respective Agency
(WTO) World Trade Organization

ACRONYMS & SOURCES

EMBASSY POSITION ABBREVIATIONS

(ADMIN) Administrative Officer
(AGR) Agricultural Officer
(CAO) Cultural Affairs Officer
(CG) Consul General
(CLO) Community Liaison Officer
(CLO ASST) Community Liaison Officer, Assistant
(COM) Commercial Officer
(CONS) Consular Officer
(CONS ASST) Consular Assistant
(CAO) Cultural Affairs Officer
(DATT) Defense Attaché
(DCM) Deputy Chief of Mission
(DS) Diplomatic Security Officer
(E/CO) Economic and Consular Officer

(ECON/COM) Economic/Commercial Officer
(ECON) Economic Officer
(ECON REP) Economic Section Representative
(FSN) Foreign Service National
(FSO) Foreign Service Officer
(IO) Information Officer
(ISM) Information Systems Manager
(MED-NUR) Medical Unit Nurse
(PERS SECY) Personnel Secretary
(PAO) Public Affairs Officer
(POL) Political Officer
(POL/ECON) Political/Economic Officer
(RSO) Regional Security Officer
(USAID DIR) USAID Mission Director
(USAID DEP) USAID Deputy Mission

SOURCES

U.S. Embassies Around the World (page 6-7): U.S. Department of State
American Presence in World Since FY 1980 (pages 8-9): U.S. State Department.
   Note: Nine countries have split capitals, but the U.S. embassy is usually based in the administrative capital. Bolivia's administrative capital is La Paz, where the U.S. embassy is located, but its legislative and judiciary center is Sucre; Cote d'Ivoire's capital is Yamoussoukro, but most government functions, including the U.S. embassy, are in the former capital of Abidjan; Germany's capital is now Berlin, but many government agencies — and the U.S. embassy — remain in Bonn; the Israeli Parliament proclaimed Jerusalem as the capital in 1950, but most embassies, including the U.S. embassy, are in Tel Aviv. Micronesia's official capital is Palikir, but all embassies, including that of the United States, remain in Kolonia, located five miles away. The capital of the Netherlands is Amsterdam, but the seat of government is The Hague, where the U.S. has its embassy. Nigeria's capital has been moved from Lagos to Abuja, but the U.S. embassy remains in Lagos. South Africa's legislative capital is Cape Town; its judiciary capital is Bloemfontein; and its administrative capital is Pretoria — home of the U.S. embassy. Swaziland's legislative capital is Lobamba and its administrative capital is in Mbabane, where the U.S. embassy is located. Although the United States does not officially recognize Taiwan as a country independent of China, many other countries do and have embassies in the capital of Taipei. The State Department acknowledges that unofficial commercial and cultural relations with the people of Taiwan are conducted through the organization, the American Institute of Taiwan, which has offices in Taipei and Kaohsiung.
Embassy Flow Chart (page 10): U.S. Department of State
A Day in the Life of an Embassy (pages 41-68): U.S. Embassy personnel, The World Almanac (1996), Encyclopedia Americana, U.S. Commerce Department, U.S. State Department, various other public documents
Embassy Profiles (page 42): The World Almanac (1996), U.S. State Department's Office of the Historian; U.S. State Department's Office of the Under Secretary for Management; U.S. Bureau of Consular Affairs; U.S. Bureau of Economic Analysis

U.S. FOREIGN SERVICE
MISSION STATEMENT

We are America's professionals in diplomacy: the Foreign Service of the United States. We advance the worldwide interests of the United States and serve and protect our fellow citizens abroad.

We provide professional non-partisan policy recommendations to the Secretary of State and the President.

We represent our country overseas and manage America's foreign relations throughout the world.

We form, along with the armed forces and the intelligence community, the triad of America's national security. We staff the front lines, working to anticipate and resolve conflicts and to attain national objectives through negotiation — and thus keep American forces out of harm's way.

We underpin and coordinate the international negotiations of specialists from all parts of our government, integrating overall national objectives.

We report and analyze international developments of concern to the United States. As students of history, languages and international relations, we are experts in cross-cultural communication and public diplomacy. We coordinate foreign assistance.

We promote United States economic and commercial interests and the export of American agricultural and industrial products and services. We stand up for American business, American workers and American investors overseas.

We champion American values: open and transparent market systems, private enterprise, the alleviation of human suffering, and economic growth in developing countries committed to their own betterment in freedom.

We advocate the ideals of the Constitution of the United States: democracy, rule of law, individual freedom and human rights.

The President and the Congress entrust us with great responsibility. We will maintain, individually and collectively, the highest standards of ethics, professionalism and loyalty.

— Proposed by AFSA Governing Board, 1996